Hot Springs and Hot Pools of the Northwest

Jayson Loam
Marjorie Gersh

AQUA THERMAL ACCESS

Hot Springs and Hot Pools of the Northwest

Revised edition: 1993

Cartography, design, layout and production by Jayson Loam

ISBN 0-9624830-5-2

Manufactured in the United States

Published by: AQUA THERMAL ACCESS
             55 Azalea Lane
             Santa Cruz, CA 95060

Front Cover Left - Pine Flats Hot Springs /136
Front Cover Right: - Upper Hot Spring /39
Back Cover: - Kah Nee Ta /80

Grateful acknowledgements to:

Staff members at state parks, national forests, national parks and hot springs resorts for their cooperation and encouragement; Diana Lindsay for identifying the benefits of having separate *Southwest* and *Northwest* regional hot spring guides; Don Haaga for his original art direction and continuing good influence; the Santa Cruz firms of Lasersmith for print-outs, Bay Photo for film processing, Dancing Man Imagery for PMTs, John Ryan for computer cover design, and Aptos Post for color separation proofs and negatives; everyone who has ever offered new information about any hot spring and all of the subjects who so graciously consented to be photographed

Photo Credits:

Bob Seal, 10, 97, 98T, 98B, 99T, 99B, 103CL, 103BL, 107T, 107R, 107B, 142T. Libbey Hot Springs Health Spa, 12B, 16T, 185T, 185R. Harrison Hotel, 17T. Phil Wilcox, 23T, 23B, 24T, 24B, 26T, 26B, 27T, 27B, 28L, 28R, 32T, 32B, 33T, 33CR, 33B, 34T, 34L, 34R, 35T, 50L, 50R, 51LT, 51LB, 51R, 56, 78, 146L, 182, 183. Tom DeLong, 25T, 25B. Chena Hot Springs, 27B. Marlene Campbell, 29T. Miette Hot Springs, 36T, 37T. Marjorie Gersh, 48, 74L. British Columbia Minestry of Forests, 49. Wellspring, 57. Town Tubs and Massage, 58T, Goldmyer Hot Springs, 59. Doe Bay Village Resort, 63. Breitenbush Hot Springs, 82T, 82B. Susan Carter, 93T, 93B, 101T, 101B, 102T, 141T, 142B, 143T, 143B. Andy Hedden-Nicely, 149. Wayne Sherr, 155. J. Russell Criswell, 167T, 168T, 169T, 169L, 170, 171T, 171B. Granite Creek Hot Springs, 167B, David Hummer, 172T, East Heaven Tub Co., 175, Crystal Spa, 176. Berkeley Springs State Park, 177L, 177R, The Greenbrier, 178L, 178R. The Homestead, 179T, 179B. Safety Harbor Spa, 183T, 183BL. Arlingon Resort Hotel, 186. Hot Springs Hilton, 187L, 187R. Elms Resort Hotel, 188. Clearwater Hot Tubs, 190. Jayson Loam, front cover, back cover and all others.

A substantial portion of the material in this book was supplied by the following Regional Contributors:

Evie Litton is a dedicated backpacker and hot springs seeker who is the author of *The Hiker's Guide to Hot Springs in the Pacific Northwest.* Copies are available for $9.95 plus $2.50 shipping from Falcon Press, P.O. Box 1718, Helena, MT 59624, or by calling toll-free (800) 582-2665.

Phil Wilcox, also known as "The Solar Man", is semi-retired and lives on a remote piece of land in Northern California. Recently returned from Canada, Alaska and Florida, he is at last report off to Mexico. When not traveling (often in search of hot springs) he designs, sells and installs remote home solar power systems. Send $3.00 for a complete solar catalog, or send SASE for basic information. The SOLAR MAN, P.O. Box 1460, Lower Lake, CA 95457.

Susan Carter lives with her husband Brian Flick in Spokane, Washington. They travel the back roads seeking and exploring little-known lakes, rivers, and hot springs of the inland northwest.

J. Russell Criswell is a member of a volunteer group which works to preserve local hot springs. He is also a part time photographer and writer whose address is 243 Sopris Avenue, Carbondale, CO. 81623. (303) 963-3573.

Bob and Glenna Seal live in the hot water "poor" section of Idaho, but spend numerous weekends driving, hiking and cross-country skiing to dip in hot springs. Together they explore central Idaho, southern Montana and western Wyoming in search of the perfect hot spring. They can be reached at 2847 St. Charles Ave., Idaho Falls, ID 83404. (208) 523-4893

Hot Springs and Hot Pools of the Northwest

Companion Volume to
Hot Springs and Hot Pools of the Southwest

Alaska
Page 22

AQUA THERMAL ACCESS

British Columbia
Page 30

Alberta
Page 31

Midwest and **Eastern States**
Page 174

Montana
Page 150

Washington
Page 52

Oregon
Page 64

Idaho
Page 86

Wyoming
Page 160

Table of Contents

Introduction   by Jayson Loam

This is a book for people to use, not an academic discussion of geothermal phenomena. For me there is a special joy and contentment which comes from soaking in a sandy-bottom pool of flowing natural mineral water, accompanied by good friends and surrounded by the peaceful quiet of a remote, primitive setting. At such an idyllic moment it is hard to get overly concerned about geology, chemistry or history. In this book it is my intent to be of service to others who also like to soak in peace and who could use some help finding just the right place.

The cataclysmic folding and faulting of the earth's crust over millions of years is a fascinating subject, especially where geologic sources have combined just the right amount of underground water with just the right amount of earth core magma to produce a hot surface flow that goes on for centuries. It would probably be fun to research and write about all that, including new data on geothermal power installations, but that is not what this book is about.

Many hot springs have long histories of special status with Indian tribes which revered the healing and peace-making powers of the magic waters. Those histories often include bloody battles with "white men" over hot spring ownership, and there are colorful legends about Indian curses that had dire effects for decades on a whole series of ill-fated owners who tried to deny Indians their traditional access to a sacred tribal spring. That, too, would be an interesting theme for a book someday, but not this book.

In the 19th century it was legal, and often quite profitable, to claim that mineral water from a famous spa had the ability to cure an impressive list of ailments. Such advertising is no longer legal, and modern medicine does not include mineral water soaks, or drinks, in its list of approved treatments. Nevertheless, quite a few people still have an intuitive feeling that, somehow, spending time soaking in natural mineral water is beneficial. I agree with the conclusion that it is "good for you", but it would take an entire book to explore all of the anecdotal and scientific material which would be needed to explain why. Someone else will have to write that book.

This book simply accepts the fact that hot springs do exist, that they have a history, and that soaking the human body in geothermal water does indeed contribute to a feeling of well-being. That still leaves several substantial practical questions. "Where can I go to legally put my body in hot water, how do I get there, and what will I find when I arrive?" The purpose of this book is to answer those questions.

When I began to design this book, I had to decide which geothermal springs would be left out because they are not "hot". Based on my own experience I picked 90 degrees as the cut-off point and ignored any hot springs or hot wells below that level, unless a commercial operator was using electricity, gas or steam to bump up the temperature of the mineral water.

The second decision I had to make was whether or not to include geothermal springs on property which was fenced and posted or otherwise not accessible to the public. There are a few hot spring enthusiasts who get an extra thrill out of penetrating such fences and soaking in "forbidden" mineral water. It was my conclusion that I would be doing my readers a major disservice if I guided them into a situation where they might get arrested or shot. Therefore, I do not provide a descriptive listing for such hot springs, but I do at least mention the names of several such well-known locations in the index, with the notation NUBP, which means "Not Usable By the Public."

And then there were several more pleasant decisions, such as whether or not to include hot wells. Technically, they are not natural hot springs, but real geothermal water does flow out of them, so, if a soaking pool is accessible to the public, I chose to include them.

Within the last 30 years the radical idea of communal soaking in a redwood or fiberglass hot tub filled with gas-heated tap water has grown into a multi-million-dollar business. Thousands of residential tubs are installed every year, all of the larger motels and hotels now have at least one, and there are now dozens of urban establishments which offer private-space hot tub rentals by the hour. I chose to include the rent-a-tub locations, which is why the basic book title is *Hot Springs **and Hot Pools***.

Early on I realized that there is no such thing as a "typical" hot spring and that there is no such thing as a "typical" hot spring enthusiast. Some readers will have a whole summer vacation to trek from one remote, primitive hot spring to another. Others will be trying to make the most of a two week vacation, a long weekend, a Saturday, or a few hours after a hard day's work. Some readers will have a self-contained RV, while others must depend on air travel and airport transportation connections. Some readers will want to find skinnydippers, while others will want to avoid skinnydippers.

Whatever your schedule, transportation and modesty needs, this book is intended to help you make an informed choice and then get you to the locations you have chosen.

Lower Loon Creek Hot Springs: One of the very best; a warm soak by a cold stream in a remote Idaho wilderness. Page 96.

Granite Creek Hot Springs: This is work? Part of our job is testing this geothermal water as it cascades into a sparkling pool built by the CCC. Page 165.

Introduction by Marjorie Gersh

When I first discovered hot springs, my old and new values were waging internal war. Therefore, I was fascinated by the Indian tradition of declaring a hot spring to be a neutral zone, devoted to peace and healing rather than to conflict, and decided to follow their lead. How wonderful it is to immerse my body in a hot spring, or even in an urban hot tub, and declare it to be my personal neutral zone.

Gathering factual information for a book about hot springs required two summers and over 15,000 miles of travel. In the process it became my personal challenge to also make a subjective evaluation of which ones "felt the best," and to observe my mental impressions of the different kinds of people who frequent the springs.

At first, I applauded almost any type of geothermal soaking pool as being a gem of natural magic. As I visited more and different springs I gradually acquired a strong preference for rustic hikes to primitive pools fed by flowing springs, and a strong prejudice against crowded commercial resorts and chlorinated pools. I noticed that some traditional resorts advertise the unique mineral analysis of their geothermal water, but I am more interested in the water being clean, comfortably warm and free from "rotten egg" odors. I especially enjoy those natural soaking pools located next to a creek where it is possible to adjust the water temperature by moving a few rocks.

During my travels I developed a theory about why natural non-commercial hot springs felt so much more relaxing than commercial resort pools. At the natural pools there is no need to "maintain an image," and almost no way to do it, especially in a group of skinnydippers. It always amazed me that sitting in the same pool might be a lawyer and his wife who had driven up from town in a Cadillac; a family touring in a motorhome; and a group traveling around the area on their motorcycles. Some of us were "barefoot all the way," others had on bathing suits. The diversity was complete. Yet, here in the warmth of the water we were all soaking together in peace. Everyone's harmonious presence complemented the quiet beauty of a remote natural hot-spring pool.

Although I live many miles from the nearest hot spring, I have the benefit of two local rent-a-tub facilities which offer outdoor communal tubs surrounded by trees, grass and flowers, and a similar diversity of people. Such an arrangement is indeed almost as good as the real thing. If you can't be at the pool you love, love the pool you're at.

9

1. Hunting for Hot Water

Goldbug Hot Springs: One variation of the ideal hot spring is a hot creek which creates a natural hot shower. Page 98.

Long before the "white man" arrived to "discover" hot springs, the Indians believed that the Great Spirit resided in the center of the earth and that "Big Medicine" fountains were a special gift from The Creator. Even during tribal battles over camping area or stolen horses, it was customary for the sacred "smoking waters" to be a neutral zone where all could freely be healed of their wounds. Way back then, hot springs did indeed belong to everyone, and understandably, we would like to believe that nothing has changed.

Most of us also have a mental picture of an ideal hot spring. It will have crystal clear water, of course, with the most beneficial combination of minerals but with no slimy algae or rotten egg smells. Water temperature will be "just right" when you first step in, as well as after you have soaked for a while. It will occupy a picturesque rock-rimmed pool with a soft sandy bottom, divided into a shallow section for lie-down soaks and a deeper section for sit-up-and-talk soaks. Naturally, it will have gorgeous natural surroundings with grass, flowers and trees, plus an inspiring view of snow-capped mountains. The location will be so remote that you have the place to yourself, and can skinnydip if you choose, but not so remote that you might get tired from a long hike. Finally, if you like to camp out, there will be a lovely campground with rest rooms conveniently nearby or, if you prefer more service, a superior motel/restaurant just a short drive down the road.

Oh yes, this ideal spring will also be located on public land and therefore belong to everyone, just like all other hot springs. That leaves only the problem of finding that ideal spring, or, better yet, lots of them.

The "good book" for hot spring seekers is the *Thermal Springs List of the United States,* published by the National Oceanic and Atmospheric Administration and available through the NOAA Environmental and Data Service office in Boulder, Colorado. This publication contains nearly 1,600 entries, with nearly all of them in the eleven western states. For each hot spring entry, latitude, longitude, water temperature and the name of the applicable USGS quadrangle map are specified. The list is accompanied by a nice big map, sprinkled with colorful location dots.

This impressive package of official information has prompted more than one desk-bound writer to recommend and/or photocopy this list, implying that there is a publicly-owned, freely-available, idyllic, primitive hot spring under every dot; just buy your USGS map and go for it. Unfortunately, the real world of geothermal water is not quite that magical. We found that only seven percent of the listed springs are on public land, accessible without charge.

Our hot springs research program did start with an analysis of the NOAA springs list. We noticed that nearly one-third of the locations had temperatures below 90º, so we eliminated them as simply not being hot enough. The other two-thirds required individual investigation, usually involving personal inspection. In addition to the above-mentioned seven percent, we found that fifteen percent were private commercial enterprises, open to the public. All the rest were on posted private property, or otherwise not usable by the public.

Space does not permit reporting all of the reasons why various springs on the NOAA list are NUBP (not usable by the public). In some cases the NOAA data is 50 or 100 years old, and the spring has simply ceased to flow due to earthquake or heavy irrigation-well pumping. Some springs have been capped and fed into municipal water systems or drowned by the construction of a water reservoir. The largest single group of NUBP springs are those on non-commercial private property. Under our public liability laws, a hot spring's owner is practically forced to either operate a commercial establishment or post the property with NO TRESPASSING signs. An owner who had graciously permitted free public use of a hot spring for years had a user hurt himself on the property, file suit against the owner and collect damages. An owner's only defense against such suits is to fence and post the property, then show that the injured person was trespassing and therefore not legally entitled to blame the owner for anything.

Among the commercial hot spring establishments there is a very wide variety of facilities and services. Each business has developed over time as a unique combination of compromises between sometimes-conflicting influences, focused around what was once a primitive hot spring. The temperature and mineral content of the geothermal water flow, and the surroundings, determined the location and original character of the business, but European traditions, Victorian prudery, medical science advances, state health department pool regulations and changing recreation patterns have affected the merchandising of that mineral water.

The Indian tradition of free access to hot springs was initially imitated by pioneering palefaces. However, as soon as mineral water was perceived to have some commercial value, the new settler's private property laws were invoked at most of the hot spring locations, and the Indians were herded off to reservations. After many fierce legal battles, and a few gun battles, some ambitious settlers were able to establish clear legal titles to the properties. Then it was up to the new owners to figure out how to turn their geothermal flow into cash flow.

Pioneering settlers dismissed as superstition the Indian's spiritual explanation of the healing power of a

Boiling River: In Yellowstone's Gardiner River, turbulent eddies provide a skin-tingling experience where hot mineral water cascades into the river. Page 169.

This Idaho commercial hot spring location used to be open to the public, but new ownership took it private, so it is now NUBP and no longer listed in the book

Fairmont Hot Springs: This quiet pool is reserved for hotel guests, who walk to it through an all-weather canopy. Page 43.

11

Kah-Nee-Tah Vacation Resort: Not all hot springs were taken from the Indians. This large commercial resort is in the Warm Springs Indian Reservation. Page 80.

Libbey Hot Springs Health Spa: This alert geothermal business offers recreational communal soaking pools on the top floor and medicare-approved physical therapy on the ground floor. Page 183.

hot spring. However, those settlers did know from experience that it was beneficial to soak their bodies in mineral water, even if they didn't know why or how it worked. Commercial exploitation began when the owner of a private hot spring first started charging admission, ending centuries of free access. Today, extracting a fee from the customer for the privilege of bathing in hot mineral water is still the fundamental transaction in the business. However, the fee you pay will seldom buy you an Indian-style soak, in a natural, free-flowing, sand-bottom hot spring in the wide open spaces. You are more likely to be offered a Victorian-style soak, in a one-person cast-iron tub in a small room in a men's or women's bathhouse, using mineral water piped in from a capped spring.

The shift from outdoor soaks to indoor soaks began when proper Victorian customers demanded privacy, which required the erection of canvas enclosures around the bathers in the outdoor springs. Then affluent city dwellers, as they became accustomed to indoor plumbing and modern sanitation, were no longer willing to risk immersion in a muddy-edged, squishy-bottom mineral spring, even if they believed that such bathing would be good for their health. Furthermore, they learned to like their urban comforts too much to trek to an outdoor spring in all kinds of weather. Instead, they wanted a civilized method of "taking the waters", and the great spas of Europe provided just the right model for American railroad tycoons and land barons to follow, and to surpass.

Around the turn of the century, American hot spring resorts fully satisfied the combined demands of Victorian prudery, modern sanitation and indoor comfort by offering separate men's and women's bathhouses, with private individual porcelain tubs, marble shower rooms and central heating. A scientific mineral analysis of the geothermal water was part of every resort merchandising program, which included flamboyant claims of miraculous cures and glowing testimonials from medical doctors. Their promotion material also featured additional social amenities, such as luxurious suites, sumptuous restaurants and grand ballrooms.

In recent decades, patronage of these resorts has declined and many have closed down because the traditional medical claims were outlawed and modern medical plans refuse to reimburse anyone for a mineral water "treatment". A few of the larger resorts have managed to survive by adding new facilities such as golf courses, conference and exhibition spaces, fitness centers and beauty salons. The smaller hot spring establishments have responded to modern demand by installing larger (six persons or more) communal soaking tubs and family-size soaking pools in private spaces for rent by the hour. Most locations continue to offer men's and women's bathhouse facilities in addition to the new communal pools, but most have discontinued the use of cast iron one-person bath tubs.

In addition to the privately-owned hot spring facilities,

there are several dozen locations which are owned by federal, state, county or city agencies. States, counties and cities usually staff and operate their own geothermal installations. However, locations in the U.S. National Forests and National Parks are usually operated under contract by privately-owned companies. The nature and quality of the mineral water facilities offered at these publicly-owned, but privately-operated, hot spring locations varies widely.

Our hunt for hot water did not stop with the NOAA hot spring list. We tracked down dozens of unintentional hot wells, resulting from oil exploration drilling, or drilling for agricultural irrigation water. Some of those hot wells have turned into "hot spring resorts", even though there never was a natural mineral hot spring at the location. There are also dozens of intentional hot wells, such as the private wells which serve motels and mobilehome parks in the Desert Hot Springs area.

Although natural mineral water (from a spring or well) is required for a truly authentic traditional "therapeutic soak", there is a new generation of dedicated soakers who will not patronize a motel unless it has a hot pool. They know full well that the pool is filled with gas-heated tap water, containing no minerals, and treated with chlorine, but it almost as good as the real thing, and a lot more convenient. Space does not permit a listing of all such motels, or hotels, or health clubs. However, we chose to include in our hunt for hot water those locations which offer private space hot tubs for rent by the hour

According to California legend, the historic redwood tub was invented by a Santa Barbara group which often visited Big Caliente Hot Springs, in the nearby mountains at the end of a Forest Service gravel road. One evening a member of the group wished out loud that they could have their delicious outdoor communal soaks without having to endure the long dusty trips to and from the springs. Another member of the group suggested that a large redwood wine cask might be used as an alternate soaking pool in the city. It would not be the real thing, but it was worth a try, and it was a success. Over time, the pioneering group discovered that their backyard redwood pool needed more than just a gas-fired water heater. It also needs a circulation pump and a filter and chlorine treatments and seats for the people. Before long, other refugees from the long Big Caliente drive began to build their own group soaking pools from wine casks, and the communal hot tub era was born.

For many years, the very idea of men and women gathering together in the same tub, especially if they didn't wear proper suits, was perceived as California-style major moral decadence and was denounced accordingly. However, as the installation of residential hot tubs gradually became a major industry nationwide, public disdain turned into public acceptance and then into public demand. Designs for many new motels now include some deluxe suites, each containing its own private hot tub, complete with tile, skimmer, hydrojets, and temperature controls.

Fountain of Youth (Sacajawea Well): While drilling for oil in 1918, wildcatters hit this million-gallons-per-day geothermal water flow. A portion of the output supplies a large swimming pool. Page 159.

Riverside Inn: This historic Idaho hot springs hotel added a California-style outdoor redwood soaking tub. Page 115.

2. Using This Guide

Pine Flats Hot Springs: Geothermal water cascading down the cliff feeds an upper pool and a cooler lower pool. Page136.

The primary tool in this guide is the KEY MAP, which is provided for each state or geographical subdivision. The KEY MAP INDEX, on the outside back cover, tells the page number where each of the KEY MAPS can be found. Each KEY MAP includes all significant cities and highways, but please note that it is designed to be used with a standard highway map.

Within every KEY MAP, each location has been assigned a number, which is imprinted next to the identifying circle or square. On the pages following the KEY MAP will be found the descriptions of each location, listed in numerical order.

The Master Alphabetical Index of Mineral Water Locations is printed at the end of the book, and gives the page number on which each location description will be found. If you know the specific hot spring name, this Alphabetical Index is the place to start.

If you are traveling in a geographical area and would like to know what hot spring or hot pool opportunities are available in that area, look at the KEY MAP for that area, note the likely location numbers and find the descriptions for those locations, by number, on the pages following the KEY MAP.

The following sections describe the quick-read symbols and codes which are used on the KEY MAPS and in the location descriptions.

Non-Commercial Mineral Water Locations

On the key maps in this book and in each hot spring listing, a solid round dot ● is used to indicate a non-commercial hot spring, or hot well, where no fee is required. At a few remote locations, you may be asked for a donation to help the work of a non-profit organization which has a contract with the Forest Service to protect and maintain the spring.

The first paragraph of each listing is intended to convey the general appearance, atmosphere and surroundings of the location, including the altitude, which can greatly affect the weather conditions. The phrase "open all year" does not mean that all roads and trails are kept open regardless of snowfalls or fire seasons. Rather, it means that there are no seasonally closed gates or doors, as at some commercial resorts.

The second paragraph describes the source and temperature of the mineral water and then conveys the manner in which that water is transported or guided to a usable soaking pool. "Volunteer-built pool" usually implies some crude combination of at-hand material such as logs, rocks and sand. If the situation requires that the pool water temperature be controlled, the method for such control is described. River-edge and creek-edge pools are vulnerable to complete washouts during high runoff months, so some volunteers have to start over from scratch every year.

The third paragraph identifies the facilities and services available on the premises, or nearby, and states the approximate distance to other facilities and services.

If needed, there is a final paragraph of directions, which should be used in connection with a standard highway map, a National Forest map if applicable, and any local area map which may be provided on the page near the listing.

With regard to skinnydipping, you had best start with the hard fact that any private property owner, county administration, park superintendent, or forest supervisor has the authority to prohibit "public nudity" in a specific area, or in a whole park or forest. Whenever the authorities have to deal with repeated complaints about nude bathers at a specific hot spring, it is likely that the area will be posted with NO NUDITY ALLOWED signs, and you could get a citation without further warning by ignoring those signs.

The vast majority of natural hot springs on public property are not individually posted, but most jurisdictions have some form of general regulation prohibiting public nudity. However, there have been some recent court cases which established the principal that a person could not be found guilty of indecent exposure if he removed his clothes only after traveling to a remote area where there was no one to be offended.

In light of these court cases, one of the largest national forests has retained its general "nude bathing prohibited" regulation, but modified its enforcement procedure to give a nude person an oportunity to put on a bathing suit before a complaint can be filed or a violation notice issued.

In practical terms, this means that a group at an unposted hot spring can mutually agree to be nude. As soon as anyone else arrives and requests that all present put on bathing suits, those who refuse that request risk a citation. If you are in the nude group, all you need from the newcomers is some tolerance. You may be pleasantly surprised at the number of people who are willing to agree to a policy of clothing-optional if, in a friendly manner, you offer them an opportunity to say "Yes."

Commercial Mineral Water Locations

On the key maps in this book and in the hot springs listings, a solid square ■ is used to indicate a natural mineral water commercial location. A phone number and mailing address are provided for the purpose of obtaining current rates, additional information and reservations.

The first paragraph of each listing is intended to convey the size, general appearance, atmosphere, and surroundings of the location, including the altitude. "Open all year" does not imply that the facility is open 24 hours of every day, only that it does not have a "closed" season.

▲ *Jerry Johnson Hot Springs:* Creekside pools offer the fun of cold-water play plus the comfort of warm water soaking. Page 88.

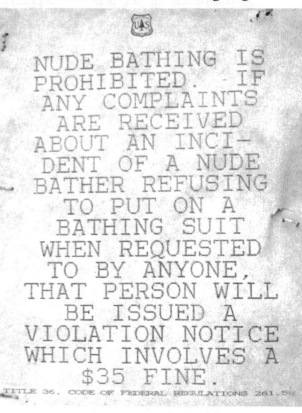

NUDE BATHING IS PROHIBITED. IF ANY COMPLAINTS ARE RECEIVED ABOUT AN INCIDENT OF A NUDE BATHER REFUSING TO PUT ON A BATHING SUIT WHEN REQUESTED TO BY ANYONE, THAT PERSON WILL BE ISSUED A VIOLATION NOTICE WHICH INVOLVES A $35 FINE.

TITLE 36. CODE OF FEDERAL REGULATIONS 261.56

▲ *Boise National Forest:* This is the new type of official notice which gives nude bathers a chance to dress before being fined.

Libbey Hot Springs Health Spa: This is one of the few mineral water rental pools available in a National Park. Page 183.

Silver Creek Plunge: Many commercial locations, such as this one, offers only a single large swimming pool. Page 138.

This book is about hot springs and hot pools where you can legally put your body in hot water. Therefore, the second paragraph of each listing focuses on the water and the pools available at the location. It describes the origin and temperature of the mineral water, the means of transporting that water, the quantity, type and location of tubs and pools, the control of soaking water temperatures, and the chemical treatment used, if any.

There actually are a few commercial locations where rare geothermal conditions (and health department rules) make it possible for a customer, or several, to soak in a natural sand-bottom hot spring open to the sky. On the other hand, there are several commercial locations which still operate separate men's and women's bathhouses fitted with traditional one-person cast-iron bathtubs. Most commercial locations fall in between these two extremes and offer a wide range of soaking opportunities.

Source hot springs are usually covered and the mineral water carried away in pipes, so customers seldom get to see a real spring, much less soak in one. Instead, the water is piped to the bathhouses for indoor use and also to swimming pools, soaking pools and hydrojet pools, usually outdoors and available for communal coed use. At a few large resorts the swimming and soaking pools may be located indoors, and some locations offer hydropools in private spaces for rent by the hour. In the last decade several resorts have also constructed special motel suites, each containing its own hydrojet pool.

In all states, health department standards require a minimum treatment of public pool water with chlorine, bromine or the equivalent. A few fortunate locations are able to meet these standards by operating their smaller mineral water pools on a continuous flow-through basis, thereby eliminating the need for chemical treatment. Many other locations meet these standards by draining and refilling tubs and pools after each use or after the end of each business day.

At those hot springs resorts which are being run as a business, bathing suits are normally required in public spaces. There are a few locations, usually operated by small special-interest groups, which have a policy of clothing-optional in the pools and sometimes everywhere on the grounds. If you are in doubt about the implications of such a policy, use the telephone to get answers to all of your questions.

The third paragraph of a commercial hot spring listing briefly mentions the principal facilities and services offered, plus approximate distances to other nearby services, and the names of credit cards accepted, if any. This information is intended to advise you if overnight accommodations, RV hookups, restaurants, health clubs, beauty salons, etc. are available on the premises, but it does not attempt to assign any form of quality rating to those amenities. There is no such thing as a typical hot spring resort and no such thing as typical accommodations at such a resort. Don't make assumptions; phone and ask questions.

For the quick-reference convenience of our readers, we

include some code letters in the headings of each listing:
PR = Tubs or pools for rent by hour, day or treatment.
MH = Rooms, cabins or dormitory spaces for rent by the day, week or month.
CRV = Camping or vehicle parking spaces, some with hookups, for rent by the day, week or month.

The PR code obviously applies to rent-a-tub establishments, and is also use for those hot springs resorts that admit the public to their pools on a day-rate basis.

The MH code covers every kind of overnight sleeping accommodation for rent, including tents and trailers as well as motel and hotel rooms, cabins and dormitories.

The CRV code is very general, indicating that there is dome kind of outdoor space in which some kind of overnight stay is possible. Some locations permit tents, most do not. Some have full hook-ups for RVs, most do not.

Tubs Using Gas-heated Tap Water or Well Water

In this book the listings of rent-a-tub locations begin with an overall impressions of the premises and the general locations, usually within a city area. This is followed by a description of their private spaces, tubs, and pools, water treatment methods, and water temperature policies. Generally, unless stated otherwise, clothing is optional in private spaces and required elsewhere. Facilities and services available on the premises are described, and credit cards accepted, if any , are listed. Nearly all locations require reservations, especially during the busy evening hours, and most employees are experienced at giving directions.

Nudist/naturist resorts which have hot pools are included as a special service to those who prefer to soak in the buff. It is true that most nudist/naturist resorts are not open to the public for drop-in visits but we wanted to give skinnydippers at least a few alternatives to all of the conventional motels/hotels/resorts which require bathing suits in all of their pools all of the time.. Most of the nudist/naturist resorts specifically prohibit bathing suits in their pools and have a policy of clothing-optional elsewhere on their grounds.

▲ *Harrison Hotel:* This is one of the larger destination resorts, offering a health pavilion, restaurant and boat rentals in addition to multiple pools. Page 46.

▲ *Heise Hot Springs:* The listing code for this commercial location includes PR for pool rental and CRV for the camping and trailer park facilities. Page 111.

17

3. Caring For The Outdoors

NATURAL HOT SPRINGS

- Water temperatures vary by site, ranging from warm to very hot . . . 180°F.

- Prolonged immersion may be hazardous to your health and result in hyperthermia (high body temperature).

- Footing around hot springs is often poor. Watch out for broken glass. Don't go barefoot and don't go alone. Please don't litter.

- Elderly persons and those with a history of heart disease, diabetes, high or low blood pressure, or who are pregnant should consult their physician prior to use.

- Never enter hot springs while under the influence of: alcohol, anti-coagulants, antihistamines, vasodilators, hypnotics, narcotics, stimulants, tranquilizers, vasoconstrictors, anti-ulcer or anti-Parkinsonian medicines. Undesirable side effects such as extreme drowsiness may occur.

- Hot springs are naturally occurring phenomena and as such are neither improved nor maintained by the Forest Service.

Bonneville Hot Springs and others: This Forest Service warning notice is posted along the unmaintained paths which lead to natural hot springs. By choosing not to improve or maintain a natural phenomena, the Forest Service is able to avoid personal injury liability suits filed by persons who ignore safety warnings, enter the area, and injure themeselves.

This is an enthusiastic testimonial and an invitation to join us in supporting the work of the U.S. Forest Service, the National Park Service, and the several State Park Services. At all of their offices and ranger stations we have always received prompt, courteous service, even when the staff was also busy handling many other daily tasks.

Nearly all usable primitive hot springs are in national forests, and many commercial hot spring resorts are surrounded by a national forest. Even if you will not be camping in one of their excellent campgrounds, we recommend that you obtain official Forest Service maps for all of the areas through which you will be traveling. Maps may be purchased from the Forest Service Regional Offices listed below. To order by mail, phone or write for an order form:

Pacific Northwest Region (503) 326-2877
Washington, Oregon
P.O. Box 3623   Portland, OR 97208

Northern Region   (406) 329-3511
Montana, Idaho, North Dakota
P.O. Box 7669   Missoula, MT 59807

Rocky Mountain Region   (303) 236-9431
Wyoming, Colorado,
Nebraska, South Dakota
P.O. Box 25127   Denver, CO 80225

Intermountain Region   (801) 625-5354
Southern Idaho, Utah,
Nevada and Western Wyoming
324 25th St.   Ogden, UT 84401

When you arrive at a national forest, head for the nearest ranger station and let them know what you would like to do in addition to putting your body in hot mineral water. If you plan to stay in a wilderness area overnight, request information about the procedure for obtaining wilderness permits and camping permits. Discuss your understanding of the dangers of water pollution, including giardia (back country dysentery) with the Forest Service staff. They are good friends as well as competent public servants.

The following material is adapted from a brochure issued by the Forest Service - Southwestern Region, Department of Agriculture.

DO NOT WASH IN STREAMS OR SPRINGS

Pour wash water on the ground away from streams and springs.

Wash yourself, your dishes and your clothes in a container, away from water sources.

Food scraps, tooth paste, even biodegradable soap will pollute streams and springs. Remember, it's your drinking water, too!

Try to pack out trash left by others. Your good example may catch on!

DON'T SHORT CUT TRAILS.

Trails are designed and maintained to prevent erosion.

PACK IT IN — PACK IT OUT

Bring trash bags to carry out all trash that cannot be completely burned.

Cutting across switchbacks and trampling meadows can create a confusing maze of unsightly trails.

Aluminum foil and aluminum lined packages won't burn up in your fire. Compact it and put it in your trash bag.

19

CAMPFIRES Use gas stoves when possible to conserve dwindliing supplies of firewood.

Use only fallen timber for firewood. Even standing dead trees are part of the beauty of wilderness, and are important to wildlife.

If you need to build a fire, use an existing campfire site if available.

Clear a circle of all burnable materials.

Dig a shallow pit for the fire.

Keep the sod intact.

If you need to clear a new fire site, select a safe spot away from rock ledges that would be blackened by smoke; away from meadows where it would destroy grass and leave a scar; away from dense brush, trees and duff where it would be a fire hazard. Keep fires small.

Never leave a fire unattended.

Put your fire COLD OUT before leaving, by mixing the coals with dirt & water. Feel it with your hand. If it's cold out, cover the ashes in the pit with dirt, replace the sod, and naturalize the disturbed area. Rockfire rings, if needed or used, should be scattered before leaving.

DON'T BURY TRASH!
Animals dig it up.

Don't pick flowers, dig up plants or cut branches from live trees. Leave them for others to see and enjoy.

BURY HUMAN WASTE

When nature calls, select a suitable spot at least 100 feet from open water, campsites and trails. Dig a hole 4 to 6 inches deep. Try to keep the sod intact.

After use, fill in the hole completely burying waste and TP: then tramp in the sod.

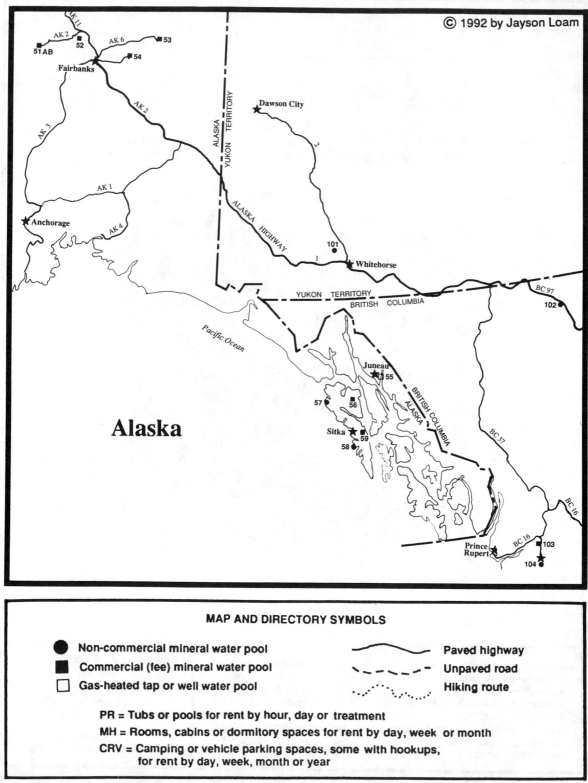

© 1992 by Jayson Loam

AK 11
AK 2
51 AB   52   AK 6   ■ 53
Fairbanks   ■ 54
AK 2
AK 3
AK 1
AK 4
Anchorage

ALASKA
YUKON TERRITORY

Dawson City

2

ALASKA HIGHWAY

101

1   Whitehorse

BC 97
YUKON   TERRITORY
BRITISH   COLUMBIA
102

Pacific Ocean

Juneau   55

57   56
BRITISH COLUMBIA
ALASKA
BC 37

Sitka   59
58

Alaska

BC 16

BC 16   103
Prince
Rupert
104

MAP AND DIRECTORY SYMBOLS

● Non-commercial mineral water pool   ∿∿∿ Paved highway

■ Commercial (fee) mineral water pool   – – – Unpaved road

□ Gas-heated tap or well water pool   ⋯⋯ Hiking route

PR = Tubs or pools for rent by hour, day or treatment

MH = Rooms, cabins or dormitory spaces for rent by day, week or month

CRV = Camping or vehicle parking spaces, some with hookups,
      for rent by day, week, month or year

▲ *Manley Hot Springs Resort:* This domed structure protects soakers and swimmers from the weather, but trees are visible at the open end, and daylight comes in through the translucent cover.

51A ■ **MANLEY HOT SPRINGS RESORT**
P.O. Box 28 (907) 672-3611
Manley Hot Springs, AK 99756
PR+MH+CRV

Rustic lodge with RV park and enclosed mineral water pools, surrounded by birch forests, 160 miles northwest of Fairbanks. Elevation 330 feet. Open all year.

Natural mineral water is pumped out of two drilled wells at 105º and piped to a translucent quonset shelter containing a plastic-lined swimming pool and a fiberglass hydropool. The swimming pool is maintained at 96º and the hydropool is maintained at 104º; both are treated with chlorine. Bathing suits are required.

Lodge rooms, restaurant, bar, RV park, laundromat, gift shop, and gasoline are available on the premises. Geothermal energy is used to heat the buildings. Visa and MasterCard are accepted.

Directions: Drive northwest from Fairbanks on AK 2. The first 28 miles are paved, the remaining 124 miles are a good dirt/gravel road. Phone ahead for winter road conditions. An airstrip is located in the town near the resort.

▲ *Manley Hot Springs:* Geothermal soaking pools are a sideline for this commercial greenhouse which grows food all year.

▼ Even on a cold artic day, *Manley Hot Springs* offers warm air and tropical foliage to go with a hot water soak.

51B   MANLEY HOT SPRINGS

■   **Manley Hot Springs, AK 99756   PR**

A unique geothermal greenhouse containing four cement soaking tubs in addition to many flowers and organic vegetables. Elevation 330 feet. Open all year.

Natural mineral water flows out of two springs (125º and 136º) and is piped to the greenhouse for space heating. and for use in the soaking pools. Temperatures of 80º, 90º, 95º, and 105º are maintained in the four pools, which are drained and refilled each day, so no chemical treatment of the water is needed. Bathing suits are required.

Note: This is primarily a commercial greenhouse enterprise, not a rent-a-tub business, so access to the tubs may not always be available. Inquire at the Post Office or at Manley Roadhouse (907) 672-3161, for current status and directions.

 Tolovana Hot Springs: Cold weather does not affect the flow of hot springs, so it is posible to soak in warm comfort while surrounded by a winter wonderland.

---

52   TOLOVANA HOT SPRINGS
P.O. Box 83058   **(907) 455-6706**
Fairbanks, AK 99708   **MH**

Two remote and rustic cabins with outdoor cedar soaking tubs, surrounded by birch and aspen forests, 100 road miles north of Fairbanks. Elevation: 800 feet. Open all year.

Natural mineral water flows out of many geothermal springs at 135° and collects in a settling pond which maintains a temperature of 100°. Water from each of these two sources is piped to the two widely-separated soaking tubs, allowing complete control of tub water temperature. The apparent local custom is clothing optional.

The two fully-outfitted cabins are the only services available on the premises. There is a remote air strip two miles from the cabins, and it is 11 miles by all-year trail to the nearest road. It is 35 miles to phone, gas and an air strip at Minto Village. Local air charters are available. Phone for guided dog sled, snow-machine or ski trips. Phone for rates, reservations and weather conditions. No credit cards are accepted.

Two miles from an airstrip, and eleven miles from the nearest road, the cabins at *Tolovana Hot Springs* offer an unusual combination of remoteness and comfort.

▲ The rustic cabins at *Circle Hot Springs* are built with logs and decorated with authentic snowshoes and moose antlers.

▲ *Circle Hot Springs:* This outdoor pool is very popular in good weather and there are eight indoor pools for other times.

---

53   **CIRCLE HOT SPRINGS**
■   **P.O. Box 254**   **(907) 520-5113**
    Central, AK 99730   **PR+MH**

Delightful historic resort hotel and cabins with a large outdoor swimming pool and several private-space hydropools, 134 miles northeast of Fairbanks. Elevation 900 feet. Open all year.

Natural mineral water flows out of a spring at 139º and is piped to an outdoor Olympic-size swimming pool and to individual hydropools in four cabins, one hydropool in the honeymoon suite and one hydropool on each of the three main floors of the hotel. The swimming pool is maintained at 105º, with a minimum of chlorination. Day use is available in the swimming pool and in the three main floor hydropools. Bathing suits are required in the swimming pool.

Hotel rooms, dining room, saloon and library are available on the premises. Geothermal energy is used to heat all rooms and cabins. It is eight miles to all other services in Central. No credit cards are accepted.

Directions: From Fairbanks, drive north on Steese Highway, then east on AK 6 to Central, and east for 8 miles on Hot Springs Road to the resort. Phone for information on rates, reservations and road conditions in winter.

▲ *Chena Hot Springs:* Heating this glassed-in swimming pool with fossil fuel would be far too expensive, but not with the free geothermal energy of a hot spring.

---

54   CHENA HOT SPRINGS

■ **P.O. Box 73440**   **(907) 452-7867**
Fairbanks, AK 99707   **PR+MH**

Comfortable lodge with cabins, an indoor swimming pool, a soaking pool and two whirlpools. Located in a wooded valley 57 miles east of Fairbanks. Elevation: 1,200 feet. Open all year.

Natural mineral water flows out of four springs at temperatures up to 156º and is piped to several pools which are treated with chlorine. The glassed-in swimming pool is maintained at 90º; the indoor soaking pool is maintained at 104º; and the two indoor whirlpools are maintained at 100º. The new pool building includes a deck containing an outdoor hydrojet pool which is maintained at 104º. All pools are available for day use as well as for registered guests. Bathing suits are required.

Hotel rooms, cabins, restaurant, and bar are available on the premises. It is 57 miles to all other services in Fairbanks. Visa, MasterCard and American Express are accepted.

Directions: From Fairbanks follow Chena Hot Springs Road (paved) east to the resort. Phone for rates and reservations.

CHENA HOT SPRINGS POOL BUILDING

▲ This is an artists sketch of the new indoor pool building, with deck and outdoor hydrojet pool, which will open for the 1993 season at *Chena Hot Springs.*

55   THE ALASKAN HOTEL

☐ 167 S. Franklin St.   (800) 327-9374
   Juneau, AK 99801   PR+MH

Hourly hot tub and sauna rentals in an historic downtown Juneau hotel. Elevation 20 feet. Open all year.

Four private-space hot pools, using gas-heated tap water, treated with   , are available for rent to the public, as well as for use by registered hotel guests. Water temperature is maintained at 102° and each space includes a sauna. The three smaller tubs will hold four persons, the larger one will hold six. Clothing is optional within the private spaces.

Rooms and a bar are available on the premises. All other services are available in the surrounding city of Juneau. Visa, MasterCard, American Express and Discover are accepted.

The hotel is located in the South Franklin National Historic Distict. Phone for rates, reservations and directions.

▲ *Tenakee Hot Springs:* In this village, unique
  bathing rules have evolved to control the
  use of a concrete pool which was built to
  protect the hot spring during high tide,
► and where buildings have been built on
  stilts to rise above high tide.

56   TENAKEE HOT SPRINGS

■   **In the town of Tenakee Springs**   PR

A wooden bathhouse containing a concrete soaking pool built over a hot spring in a tiny rural Alaskan village with no cars or roads. Elevation is at sea level. Open all year.

Natural mineral water flows out of the spring at 108°, directly up into a 5' by 10' concrete container which was built to keep out the sea water at high tide. Men and women are assigned different hours of the day. Bathing suits and soap are prohibited in the pool. Donations are accepted in the adjoining store.

There are no services available on the premises, but rooms, bunkhouse, bar and laundry are offered nearby in the nostalgic victorian Tenakee Inn. (800) 327-9347. A restaurant and curio shop are located nearby.

The Alaska Marine Highway Ferry stops for only fifteen minutes at Tenakee Springs, which is located on the north shore of Tenakee Inlet on Chichagof Island, 45 miles southwest of Juneau.

57   WHITE SULPHUR HOT SPRINGS

● **Northwest of the city of Sitka   MH**
Remote hot spring pools, with a nearby rentable National Forest Service cabin, within a wilderness area of Tongass National Forest, 65 miles from Sitka. Elevation 50 feet. Open all year.

Natural mineral water flows out of one spring at 111º, supplying a natural-bottom primitive soaking pool. A three-sided log structure with a concrete soaking pool has been built directly over another spring. The open side of this shelter provides a spectacular view of Pacific Ocean waves crashing on rocky cliffs. The apparent local clothing custom is the mutual agreement of those present.

For cabin reservation information contact the U.S. Forest Service, 204 Siginaka Way, Sitka, AK 99835. (907) 747-6671. There are no other services available on the premises. Access is only by boat, plus a one-mile hike from Mirror Harbor. For additional information and charter boat service, contact the sources noted in the Goddard Hot Springs listing.

▲ *White Sulphur Hot Springs:* Volunteers have used rocks and a little cement to preserve the charm of this primitive pool.

58   GODDARD HOT SPRINGS

● **South of the city of Sitka   CRV**
Two modern cedar soaking tubs in open shelters overlooking beautiful Hot Springs Bay on the outer coast of Baranof Island. Elevation 30 feet. Open all year.

Natural mineral water flows out of a spring at 153º and is piped to a double faucet on each tub. Cold water is also piped to that faucet, permitting complete control over the tub water temperature. There is no charge for using the facilities, which are owned and maintained by the City of Sitka. The apparent local clothing custom is by mutual agreement of those present.

Boardwalks and stairs have been constructed and campsites are located nearby. There are no other services available on the premises. Access is possible only by boat. For more information contact the Sitka Convention and Visitors Bureau, P.O. Box 1226 Sitka, AK 99835. (907) 747-5940, and for boat charter service contact Alaskan Waters Unlimited, (907) 747-5777.

▲ *Goddard Hot Springs:* Most non-commercial hot springs are rather primitive but here the City of Sitka has provided modern cedar tubs, a shelter and a view.

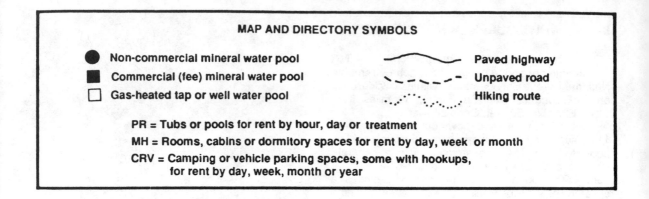

This map was designed to be used with a standard highway map

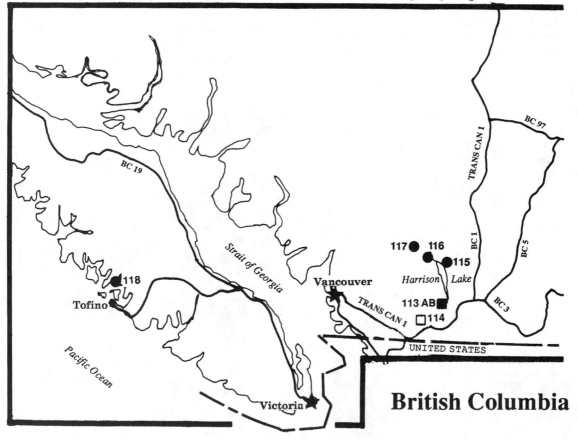

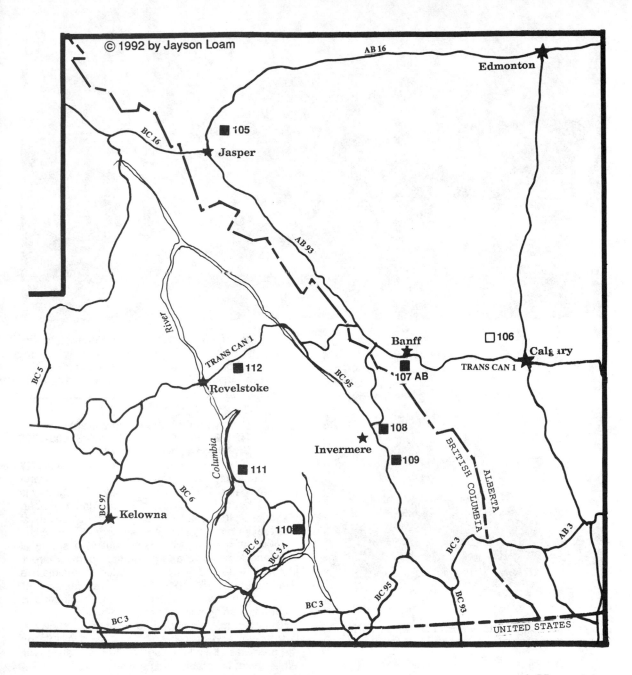

© 1992 by Jayson Loam

AB 16

Edmonton

BC 16

■ 105

Jasper

AB 93

River

Banff

□ 106

Calgary

TRANS CAN 1

BC 5

■ 112

Revelstoke

BC 95

107 AB

TRANS CAN 1

Columbia

■ 108

Invermere

■ 109

BRITISH COLUMBIA

ALBERTA

■ 111

BC 6

AB 3

BC 97

Kelowna

110 ■

BC 3

BC 6

BC 3 A

BC 3

BC 95

BC 93

BC 3

UNITED STATES

Alberta

Forested hills extend for miles in all directions from *Takhini Hot Springs.*

Takhini Hot Springs: No one has to shiver through cold air getting to this swimming pool because warm pool water extends well up into the enclosed walkway structure.

101   TAKHINI HOT SPRINGS
■   (shown on the Alaska key map)
RR #2, Site 19, Comp 4   (403) 633-2706
Whitehorse, Yukon, Y1A 5A5

PR+MH+CRV

Restaurant, campground, and mineral water pool in scenic Takhini River valley. Daylight runs from 19 hours in June to 5 1/2 hours in December. Elevation 2,400 feet. Open all year, but closed most weekdays from October 1 to February 28.

Natural mineral water flows out of a spring at 118º and is piped to a large outdoor pool, where it is mixed with cold water as needed to maintain a temperature of 102-104º. The pool is drained and refilled each day, so a minimum of chlorination is required. Bathing suits are required.

Restaurant, campground, sauna, showers, laundromat and horseback riding are available on the premises. It is 17 miles to all other services in Whitehorse. No credit cards are accepted.

Directions: Northwest of Whitehorse on the Alaska Highway, turn north on YT 2 toward Dawson City. Drive 3 miles, then watch for Takhini Hot Springs sign and turn west 6 miles to the springs.

102 LIARD HOT SPRINGS PROVINCIAL PARK
(shown on the Alaska key map)
Northwest of Muncho Lake, BC   CRV

A lovely, primitive geothermal pond and pool, with convenient boardwalk access and a campground, adjoining the Alaska Highway near the Yukon border. Elevation 1,500 feet. Open all year.

Natural mineral water flows out of several springs at temperatures up to 120º directly into a large shallow natural pond (named Alpha) created by a low dam across the creek bed. The water cools to comfortable levels as it flows toward the spillway over the dam. Underwater benches are provided for soaking convenience, and the shallow end of the pond is suitable for children. One side of the pond has been improved with stairs, a large deck, changing rooms and toilets. A six-foot-wide boardwalk has been built through a wetlands environment from the parking area to the pond.

Five minutes beyond Alpha, along a dirt path, is a large natural pool (named Beta) which maintains a temperature of more than 100º. It also has stairs, a small deck, changing rooms and toilets, but is used primarily by adults because of the deep water.

There is no charge for day use of the pools, but a fee is charged for sites in the campground. During the popular summer months, campsites fill early in the day. There are no other services available on the premises. There is a cafe across the highway and a lodge within 1/2 mile. It is 41 miles to all other services. No credit cards are accepted.

The park is located at mile marker 497 (765 km) on the Alaska Highway (BC 97) just below the Yukon Territory border. Follow the signs prominently displayed along the highway.

Liard Hot Springs Provincial Park (Alpha Pool): A low dam was built to turn a mud wallow into an enjoyable natural soak.

The nearby *Beta Pool* at *Liard Hot Springs Provincial Park* is cooler, deeper and less popular than the entrancing Alpha Pool.

Mount Layton Hot Springs Resort: This modern new destination resort plans to add both a golf course and an RV park.

This single tower provides an indoor stairway to three different water slides.

Two of the *Mount Layton* water slides have an indoor catch pool so the fun can continue independent of the weather.

▲ Children too small for the big *Mount Layton* water slide tubes have their own slides at the shallow end of the pool.

103 MOUNT LAYTON HOT SPRINGS RESORT
(shown on the Alaska key map)

P.O. Box 550	**(604) 798-2214**
Terrace, BC V8G 4B5	**PR+MH**

A large new 1,000-acre destination resort and water park in a beautiful setting on the edge of Lakelse Lake in Western British Columbia. Elevation: 800 feet. Open all year.

Natural mineral water flows out of several springs at temperatures up to 186º, is treated with ozone, and then piped to various pools and waterslides without requiring any other chemical treatment. The outdoor therapeutic pool is maintained at 103º and the outdoor main pool is maintained at 90º. Two of the three big waterslides exit into an indoor catch pool which is maintained at 90º. The third big waterslide exits outdoors into an arm of the main pool. There are also two short outdoor waterslides suitable for small children. Bathing suits are required.

Hotel rooms, restaurant, bar and snack room are available on the premises. Fishing and boating are available at adjoining Lakelse Lake. (Future development plans include an RV park and a golf course. Phone ahead for information on the status of construction.) It is 10 miles to all other services in Terrace. Visa, MasterCard, Diners, and American Express are accepted.

Directions: From Terrace, drive 14 miles south on BC 37 to the resort.

104 DOUGLAS CHANNEL HOT SPRINGS
● **(shown on the Alaska key map)**

Eight different natural hot spring sites, some partially improved, along the edges of beautiful Douglas Channel. Accessible only by boat. Elevation: sea level. Open all year.

The three most popular sites are:

Bishop Bay; One spring, 110º, fifteen feet above high tide, supplies a 3-foot by 3-foot concrete bathhouse. Mooring buoys and a dock are also in place.

Weewanie; one spring, 117º, 330 feet above sea level, supplies a small cement bathhouse, built with a grant from Crown Zellerbach.

Shearwater Point; Several springs, 113º, in a fractured rock wall, supply a brick pool built by a lumber company for its employees in 1922.

The other sites are difficult to find and/or are flooded at high tide. For more information, contact the Kitimat Chamber of Commerce, P.O. Box 214, Kitimat, BC V8C 2G7. (604) 632-6294, FAX (604) 632-4685.

Directions: Kitimat is at the head of Douglas Channel, 36 miles south of Terrace on BC 37.

Miette Hot Springs: Thanks to a modernization program, with new pools and bathhouses, this installation is among the finest in the Parks Canada system.

105 MIETTE HOT SPRINGS
Jasper National Park Box 10
Jasper, AB T0E 1E0 Canada   PR+MH

A modern, clean and proper, Canadian Pars Service communal plunge in a remote part of beautiful Jasper National Park. Elevation 4,500 ft. Open mid-May to Labor Day.

Natural mineral water flows out of several springs at temperatures up to 129º and is piped to two outdoor pools where it is treated with chlorine and maintained at approximately 104º. Bathing suits are required and can be rented at the facility.

Locker rooms are available on the premises. A cafe, motel and cabins are available nearby. It is 11 miles to a store, service station and overnight camping and 15 miles to RV hookups. No credit cards are accepted.

Directions: From the town of Jasper, drive 42km (26 miles) north on AB 16, then follow signs southeast to the springs.

▲ One of the many attractions at *Miette Hot Springs* is that smoking is prohibited in the pool area and related buildings.

▼ *Sunny Chinooks Family Nudist Park:* This hydropool is indoors but growing plants in pots give it a tropical feel.

106   SUNNY CHINOOKS FAMILY NUDIST RECREATIONAL PARK
☐   P.O. Box 33030   (403) 640 4606
       Calgary, AB T3E 7E2   PR+MH+CRV

Rustic and secluded nudist park on 40 wooded acres, an hour's drive from Calgary. Elevation 4,500 ft. Open May through September.

Gas-heated well water is used in an indoor hydropool maintained at 102-104º and treated with chlorine. Gas-heated well water is also used in an outdoor swimming pool maintained at 80º and treated with chlorine. Clothing is always prohibited in the pools and, weather permitting, prohibited everywhere on the grounds.

A cafe, convenience store, cabin and trailer rentals, overnight camping and RV hookups are available on the premises. It is 17 miles to a service station. No credit cards are accepted.

Note: This is a membership organization not open to the public for drop-in visits, but prospective members may be issued a guest pass by prior arrangement. Telephone or write for information and directions.

107A UPPER HOT SPRING

Banff National Park Box 900
Banff, AB T0L 0C0   **PR**

A modern, clean and proper, Parks Canada communal plunge surrounded by the beautiful scenery of Banff National Park. Elevation 5,000 ft. Open all year.

Natural mineral water flows out of a spring at temperatures ranging from 90-108º, depending on snow run-off conditions, and is piped to an outdoor swimming pool where it is treated with chlorine. Water temperature in the swimming pool is slightly lower than the current spring output temperature. Bathing suits are required.

Locker rooms are available on the premises. It is one mile to a cafe, store, and motel, and four miles to overnight camping and RV hookups. No credit cards are accepted.

Directions: From the south end of Banff Avenue, follow signs to the spring.

◀ *Upper Hot Spring:* The outflow temperature of the spring feeding this pool is affected by snow run-off.

107B CAVE AND BASIN HOT SPRING

Banff National Park Box 900
Banff, AB, T0L 0C0   **PR**

A modern, clean and proper, Parks Canada communal plunge within the Cave and Basin Centennial Centre, surrounded by the beautiful mountain scenery of Banff National Park. Elevation 4,200 ft. Pool open during summer months. Free exhibits open all year.

Natural mineral water (95º) flows out of the Cave and the Basin Hot Springs, which are for viewing only. The water is then piped to a large outdoor swimming pool, which is chlorinated, maintains a temperature of approximately 90º, and is available for public use. Bathing suits are required and historic costumes are available for rent.

Locker rooms and a restaurant are available on the premises. It is one mile to a store, service station and hotel rooms, and three miles to overnight camping and RV hookups. No credit cards are accepted.

Directions: From the south end of Banff Avenue, follow signs to the spring.

 Cave and Basin Hot Spring: A decorative wall with windows is used to keep the wind out while letting the scenery in.

Radium Hot Spring: The Aquacourt area at this popular Parks Canada installation has a convenient observation deck and a restaurant in addition to dressing rooms.

MAP AND DIRECTORY SYMBOLS

● Non-commercial mineral water pool

■ Commercial (fee) mineral water pool

☐ Gas-heated tap or well water pool

〜〜〜 Paved highway

— — — Unpaved road

∙∙∙∙∙ Hiking route

PR = Tubs or pools for rent by hour, day or treatment

MH = Rooms, cabins or dormitory spaces for rent by day, week or month

CRV = Camping or vehicle parking spaces, some with hookups,
for rent by day, week, month or year

---

108 RADIUM HOT SPRINGS

P.O. Box 220   (604) 347-9485
Radium Hot Springs, BC V0A 1M0
PR+MH+CRV

A modern, clean and proper, Canadian Parks Service communal plunge with adjoining commercial services, surrounded by the beautiful mountain scenery of Kootenay National Park. Elevation 2,800 ft. Open all year.

Natural mineral water flows out of five springs at a combined temperature of 114º and is piped to two outdoor pools where it is treated with chlorine. The swimming pool is maintained at a temperature of 83º, and the soaking pool is maintained at a temperature of 98-103º. Bathing suits are required.

Locker rooms, massage and a cafe are available on the premises, with rooms, overnight camping and RV hookups available nearby. It is two miles to a store and service station. No credit cards are accepted.

Directions: Follow signs one mile east from the West Gate of Kootenay National Park.

► Some of the rooms in the nearby lodge have a spectacular view of the landscaped pools at *Radium Hot Springs.*

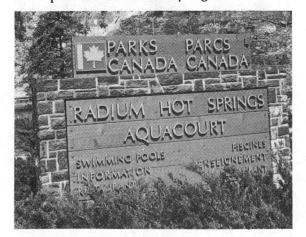

▲
► *Fairmont Hot Springs Resort:* A large
fenced area encloses the lawn, pools and
bathhouse available for day-use. The
prominent sign on the fence makes it clear
that you will need a swim suit and that
you will need to bring your own.

NOTICE
DUE TO HEALTH REGU-
LATIONS, NO ONE IS
ALLOWED WITHIN POOL
ENCLOSURE UNLESS
ATTIRED FOR SWIMMING
*RENTAL SWIM SUITS
NOT AVAILABLE*

109 FAIRMONT HOT SPRINGS RESORT

P.O. Box 10   (604) 345-6311
■   **Fairmont Hot Springs, BC V0B 1L0**
                             PR+MH+CRV

Famous, large, destination resort and communal plunge, beautifully landscaped and surrounded by the forested mountains of the Windermere Valley. Elevation 2,100 ft. Open all year.

Natural mineral water flows out of three springs at temperatures of 108º, 112º, and 116º and is piped to the resort pools where it is treated with chlorine and cooled with creek water as needed. The outdoor public plunge area includes a swimming pool maintained at 100º, a soaking pool maintained at a temperature of 102-104º, an indoor soaking pool maintained at 106º, and a cold plunge maintained at 60º. The lodge also has two co-ed saunas. Bathing suits are required.

Locker rooms, massage, cafe, store, service station, hotel rooms, overnight camping (no tents), RV hookups, saddle horses, tennis, golf and skiing are available on the premises. Visa, MasterCard and American Express are accepted.

Location: On BC 93, 64 miles north of Cranbrook and 100 miles south of Banff.

▲ Registered overnight guests at *Fairmont Hot Springs Resort* have their own separate pool and walk to it through an all-weather sheltered walkway.

Ainsworth Hot Springs: Source springs in the caves maintain steambath-like heat. The outdoor soaking pool and swimming pool have more comfortable levels.

110   AINSWORTH HOT SPRINGS
P.O. Box 1268   (604) 229-4212
Ainsworth Hot Springs BC V0G 1A0
PR+MH

Modern, all-year destination resort with a multi-pool plunge and geothermal caves, overlooking beautiful Kootenay Lake. Elevation 1,900 ft. Open all year.

Natural mineral water flows out of five springs at temperatures ranging from 110-117º. The outdoor swimming pool and connected hydrojet pool are maintained at 85-95º. The water in the caves ranges from 106-110º and is circulated to the connected outdoor soaking pool, where it ranges from 104-106º. There is a ledge in the cave which may be used as a steambath. There is also an outdoor cold pool containing creek water ranging from 40-60º. All pools are treated with chlorine. Bathing suits are required.

Facilities include hotel rooms, lounge, dining room, banquet rooms, meeting rooms and dressing rooms. Massage, by appointment, is available on the premises. It is 1/2 mile to overnight camping and nine miles to a store and service station. MasterCard, Visa and Diners Club are accepted.

Location: On BC 31, 12 miles south of Kaslo and 29 miles from Nelson.

▲ *Nakusp Hot Springs:* These town-owned pools are for relaxed social soaking. There is no deep end for diving.

▲ *Canyon Hot Springs:* Even the smaller commercial resorts in the area enjoy snow-capped mountain scenery.

---

111 NAKUSP HOT SPRINGS

P.O. Box 280	(604) 265-4528
Nakusp, BC V0G 1R0	PR+MH+CRV

Modern, clean, city-owned plunge, with creekside camping spaces surrounded by beautiful mountain scenery. Elevation 2,200 ft. Open all year.

Natural mineral water flows out of springs at 135º and is piped to two outdoor pools where it is treated with chlorine. The swimming pool is maintained at 100º and the soaking pool at 110º. Bathing suits are required.

Locker rooms, cabins and overnight camping are available on the premises. It is eight miles to a cafe, store, service station and RV hookups. Visa cards are accepted.

Directions: From a junction on BC 23 one mile north of Nakusp, follow signs eight miles east to the plunge.

112 CANYON HOT SPRINGS

P.O. Box 2400	(604) 837-2420
Revelstoke, BC V0E 2S0	PR+CRV

Well-kept commercial plunge with creekside camping spaces, surrounded by the beautiful scenery below Glacier National Park. Elevation 3,000 ft. Open May 15 to September 15.

Natural mineral water flows out of a spring at 85º and is gas-heated as needed, as well as being treated with chlorine. The outdoor swimming pool is maintained at 85º and the outdoor soaking pool at 105º. Bathing suits are required.

Locker rooms, cafe, store, RV hookups and overnight camping are available on the premises. It is 21 miles to a service station and motel. Visa, MasterCard and American Express are accepted.

Location: 21 miles east of Revelstoke on Canada 1.

The Harrison Hotel: This full-service resort hotel provides a buffet lunch and bar service at the main swimming pool.

Convivial sing-a-longs make the rafters ring in this hot pool building adjoining the main pool at *The Harrison Hotel.*

113 A   THE HARRISON HOTEL

(604) 521-8888
Harrison Hot Springs, BC V0M 1K0
PR+MH

Attractive, large, destination resort located on the south shore of beautiful Lake Harrison. This well-managed facility offers an unusually wide range of recreation activities. Elevation 47 ft. Open all year.

Natural mineral water flows out of a spring at 140º and is piped to cooling tanks before being treated with chlorine. The Olympic-size outdoor swimming pool is maintained at 82º, the indoor swimming pool at 94º, and the indoor soaking pool at 104º. The men's and women's sections of the health pavilion each contain a Roman bath in which the temperature is controllable. Health pavilion services are available to the public, but all other facilities are reserved for registered guests only. Bathing suits are required.

Future development plans include four large outdoor soaking pools with connecting waterfalls and temperatures ranging from 110º down to 85º, two outdoor chlorine-treated fresh water swimming pools ranging in temperature from 78-82º, and a swimway connecting the indoor swimming pool with the outdoor swimming pool. Plans for the health pavilion include mud baths, fitness center and weight room, herbal wraps, etc. Phone ahead to determine the status of construction.

A restaurant, bungalows, rooms, children's programs, pickle ball, boat cruises and boat rentals are available on the premises. It is three blocks to a store, service station, overnight camping and RV hookups. Visa, MasterCard, American Express, Enroute and Discover are accepted.

Location: 65 miles east of Vancouver at the south end of Lake Harrison. Phone for rates, reservations and additional directions.

Harrison Hot Springs Public Pool: The same hot spring which supplies mineral water to the hotel two blocks away also supplies this well-kept plunge.

113B HARRISON HOT SPRINGS PUBLIC POOL

c/o Harrison Hotel
Harrison Hot Springs, BC V0M 1K0   PR

Large, modern, indoor communal plunge owned and operated by the hotel, available to the public. Elevation 47 ft. Open all year.

Natural mineral water is drawn from the same spring that supplies the hotel. It is treated with chlorine and maintained at 100º in the swimming pool. Bathing suits are required.

Locker rooms are available on the premises. All other services are within three blocks. Visa and MasterCard are accepted.

Location: On the main intersection at the beach in Harrison Hot Springs.

114   SUNNY TRAILS CLUB

Box 18, 43955 #7 Highway (604) 826-3419
Lake Errock, B.C. V0M 1N0   PR+CRV

An ideal northwest nudist park with 18 acres of trees and grass, including 50 campsites, conveniently located 1 1/2 hours from downtown Vancouver. Elevation 700 ft. Open all year.

Gas-heated spring water is used in an enclosed fiberglass hydropool which is maintained at 104º, and in an outdoor, unheated swimming pool, both of which are treated with chlorine. Bathing suits are prohibited in the pools.

Facilities include a sauna, cafe, children's playground, overnight camping, RV hookups, and laundry facilities. It is five miles to a store, service station and motel. No credit cards are accepted.

Note: This is a membership nudist organization and only INF/ASA members have unlimited access. Non-members have a maximum of four daytime visits per year with no overnight priviledges, but they are most welcome to come and visit our park. Telephone or write for information and directions.

Most hot springs visitors patronize those convenient and comfortable establishments which offer tiled pools, hot showers, a restaurant and a souvenir shop, with nearby overnight accommodations. However, a hardy minority make a point of seeking out those remote and primitive hot springs which are inconvenient and, at times, inaccessible.

Many of them are on or near logging roads, which means that quite often public access is prohibited between 6 am and 6 pm during logging season, and that the road could be closed by slides, washouts, snow, high fire danger, and actual forest fires. In other words, access to primitive and remote hot springs is a sometimes thing.

Therefore, the best first step toward reaching any remote hot spring is to contact the Provincial Ministry of Forests District Office for the area and inquire about current conditions. Then, if access is possible, you can obtain an official map, a current weather report, and first hand directions. The office hours are from 8:30 am to 4:30 pm, Monday through Friday.

▼ *Skookumchuck Hot Springs:* Volunteers have piped continuously-running hot and cold water to this oversize plastic tub.

115 SKOOKUMCHUCK HOT SPRINGS (LILLOOET) (ST. AGNES WELL)
● South of the town of Pemberton, BC

Two large, fiberglass soaking tubs in a small clearing near a logging road along the Lillooet River. Elevation 100 ft. Open all year; however, the road is not plowed in winter.

Natural mineral water flows out of a spring at 129º. Volunteers have mounted the two halves of a fiberglass storage tank near the springs, using long pieces of PVC pipe to bring a gravity flow of hot mineral water. Other pieces of PVC pipe are used to carry a gravity flow from a cold-water spring. Water temperature within each tub is controlled by mixing the hot and cold water. One of the tubs is in the open; the other is under a crude A-frame shelter. In the absence of posted rules, the use of bathing suits is determined by the consent of those present.

There are no services available, but there are numerous nearby self-maintained camping areas along the logging road and at the site itself.

Directions: From the town of Mt. Currie, go approximately 34 miles on a rough logging road along the Lillooet River. At BC Hydro tower #682, turn right onto a camping-area access road and go 1/4 mile to spring. Caution: this dirt road may require a 4-wheel-drive vehicle when wet.

The hot springs are located on private property, and use is permissible without the consent of the property owner. Please respect the hot springs and adjacent property. Pack out all garbage.

▲ *Clear Creek Hot Springs:* Some volunteers were willing to truck in a wooden tub to avoid soaking in a squishy-bottom pool.

116   SLOQUET CREEK HOT SPRINGS

● **Near the north end of Harrison Lake, BC**

Several springs seep from the rocks about Sloquet Creek and flow along the ground before dropping over a short waterfall and forming a small pool which is too hot for bathing. Several other springs percolate from the ground, and volunteers have constructed small, natural-rock pools for bathing along the creek. The hot springs are located about 62 miles south of Mt. Currie, near the Lillooet River and just northwest of Harrison Lake. Elevation approximately 1000 ft. Water temperature varies between 135º and 155º.

Few services are available in the area, though there is a logging camp at Port Douglas, at the head of Harrison Lake. Walk-in camping is possible near the springs.

Directions: From the town of Mt. Currie, go about 57 miles south on the logging road along the Lillooet River to a bridge that crosses the river to the west side. Turn left, cross Fire Creek, and go south two miles to a second creek, where you go right. Follow this creek (Sloquet) for about 3.4 miles on an old logging road that takes you to a bridge across North Sloquet Creek. The bridge is washed out and you must cross the creek on foot via a large log. Follow the logging road until you reach an obvious clearing that can be used for camping. There is a trail leading downhill from the clearing to the creek and the hot springs. It will take two to three hours to drive from Mt. Currie and an additional 45 minutes to walk the remainder of the logging road to the hot springs. There are no posted rules or regulations for use of the site, but anything packed in should be packed out, including garbage.

117   CLEAR CREEK HOT SPRINGS

● **Along the northeast side of Harrison Lake, BC**

Two small wooden tubs and two old porcelain bathtubs are located near a log cabin along Clear Creek, approximately 35 miles up the east side of Harrison Lake from Harris Hot Springs, and six miles east of the lake up Clear Creek. Elevation approximately 2,200 ft. Hot springs open all year; however, road passable only in summer and only to 4x4's. A spring percolates from the ground at 95º, and volunteers have constructed two wooden tubs connected to the springs with long lengths of PVC pipe. There are two conventional bathtubs which can also be used for soaking.

There are few amenities available in the area other than the log cabin and an outhouse nearby. The springs are located on an active mineral claim which was initially prospected by a woman who built the cabin and an Olympic-sized swimming pool about 15 years ago. The pool is largely filled with algae and silt and not used by bathers any longer.

Directions: From the town of Harrison Hot Springs head up the east side of Harrison Lake for about 33 miles to the logging camp at Big Silver Creek. Stay on the main logging road for another five miles and look for a narrow road going off to the right. This is the old mining road up Clear Creek, and it is extremely rough in places. It is driveable with a narrow 4x4 for most of the six miles to the hot springs and cabin, which are located on the right side of the creek. It will take two-to-three hours to drive from Harrison Hot Springs to the Clear Creek road, and considerably longer if you walk up the road. There are no posted rules or restrictions for use of the site, but anything packed in should be packed out, including garbage.

Most of the soaking pools at *Hot Springs Cove* are primitive and rather small.

118   HOT SPRINGS COVE

● **Northwest of the town of Tofino,
on Vancouver Island**

Unique confluence of geothermal run-off and ocean waves, located in Maquinna Regional Park on a rocky peninsula reachable only by boat or floatplane. Elevation 40 ft. Open all year.

Natural mineral water flows out of the main spring at 122º, providing a hot showerbath as it falls over a cliff edge. This geothermal water gradually cools as it flows through a series of soaking pools in a rocky channel leading to the ocean. The incoming tide and wave action intermittently splash cold sea water over the visitors in the lower pools. Clothing optional is the apparent local custom. The remoteness of this location does not assure you of privacy. During summer weekends, you will have plenty of company, which insures a maximum of excitment when the icy waves surge into the tubs.

There are no facilities or services on the premises. It is one mile on a cedar-board walk to a fishing-boat dock with a quaint small store usually open for snacks, soft drinks, etc. Overnight camping near the springs is not prohibited. Rooms are available in the lodge at a nearby Indian village. For rates and resevations contact Inter Island Excursions, 71 Wharf Street., Tofino, B.C. V0R 2Z0, CANADA. (604) 725-3163.

The most convenient access, weather permitting, is by boat or floatplane out of Tofino, 23 miles south of Hot Springs Cove. Inter Island Excursions (see above) provides Zodiac boat service to the Cove and for whale watching along the way.

▲ *Hot Springs Cove:* During high tide the lower end of this hot spring run-off channel is splashed with breaking waves, which stimulate a chorus of screaming.

▲ An easy cedar-board walk leads toward *Hot Spring Cove* from the dock, but the last few yards require some rock scrambling.

▲ *Hot Spring Cove* may be a long way from a city, but the hot showers run all day.

▼ Access to *Hot Springs Cove* is from this fishing-boat dock one mile away.

MANITOU SPRINGS MINERAL SPA
(not shown on any key map)
■ P.O. Box 967   (306) 946-3949
Manitou Beach, SK S0K 4T0   PR+MH

Large new resort hotel and spa featuring indoor pools filled with mineral-rich water pumped from adjoining Little Manitou Lake, located 70 miles southeast of Saskatoon. Elevation 500 feet. Open all year.

Lake-bottom mineral springs supply the lake with water three times saltier than the ocean. This highly bouyant water is pumped to three indoor pools, where it is heated with gas and treated with chlorine. The exercise pool is maintained at 94º, the soaking cove is maintained at 98º, and the water massage pool is maintained at 100º. Bathing suits are required.

Hotel rooms, restaurant, bar, gift shop, retail mall, and massage are available on the premises. It is three miles to a service station and a store. Visa and MasterCard are accepted.

Directions: From the town of Watrous, 70 miles southeast of Saskatoon, drive three miles north on SK 365 to Manitou Beach and follow signs to the Spa.

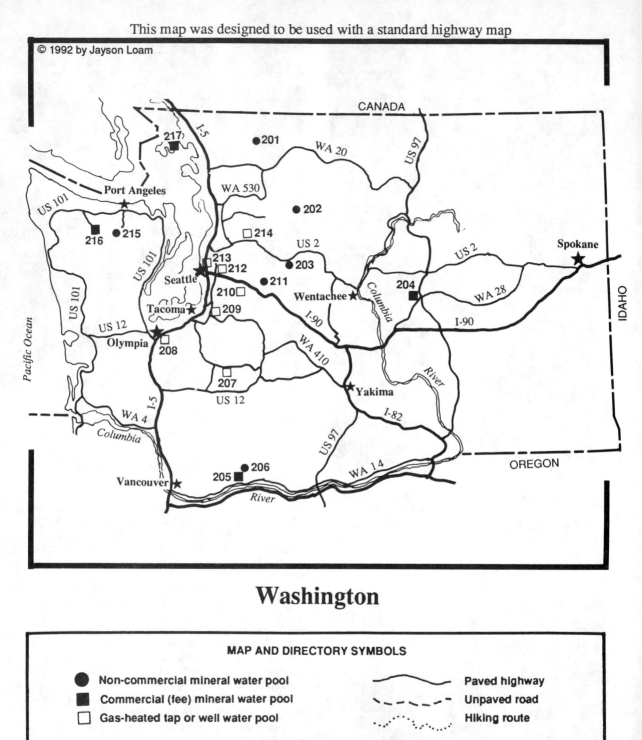

© 1992 by Jayson Loam

Washington

MAP AND DIRECTORY SYMBOLS

● Non-commercial mineral water pool

■ Commercial (fee) mineral water pool

□ Gas-heated tap or well water pool

〜〜〜 Paved highway

– – – – Unpaved road

········· Hiking route

PR = Tubs or pools for rent by hour, day or treatment

MH = Rooms, cabins or dormitory spaces for rent by day, week or month

CRV = Camping or vehicle parking spaces, some with hookups,
       for rent by day, week, month or year

201 BAKER HOT SPRINGS

● **North of the town of Concrete**

Charming, primitive spring located at the end of an easy 600-yard path through the lush, green timber of Mt. Baker National Forest. Elevation 2,000 ft. Open all year, day use only.

Natural mineral water bubbles up into the bottom of a large, round, volunteer-built pool at 109°. Water temperature in this sandy-bottom pool is controlled by admitting or diverting the water from a small, adjacent cold stream. The apparent local custom is clothing optional. Conscientious visitors have kept the area litter free. Please help to maintain this standard.

There are no facilities on the premises, and no overnight camping is permitted. However, there is a Forest Service campground within three miles. All other services are located 20 miles away, in Concrete.

Directions: From WA 20, five miles east of Hamilton, turn north on Grandy Creek Road toward Baker Lake. Just beyond Park Creek Campground, near the head of the lake, go left on FS 1144, and after 3.2 miles, watch for an unusually large parking area on both sides of the gravel road. (If you reach a U-turn to the left with a branch road going off to the right, you have gone too far.) An unmarked trail to the hot springs starts with wood steps which are visible at the north end of the parking area on your left. Follow the easy trail west to the spring.

Source map: *Mt. Baker-Snoqualmie National Forest* (hot spring not shown).

▲ *Baker Hot Springs:* Until several years ago the outflow from this spring was piped into a redwood hot tub. However, bacteria grew in that tub because the flow rate was too low, so the health department condemned it, and the Forest Service had to destroy it. This volunteer-built natural-bottom pool does not have a bacteria build-up problem.

202   KENNEDY HOT SPRING

● **Southeast of the town of Darrington**

A popular scenic hot spring, five miles in on a trail that connects with the Pacific Crest Trail one mile father on. Located in a rugged canyon of the White Chuck River in the Glacier Peak Wilderness. Elevation 3,300 ft. Open all year.

Natural mineral water flows out of a spring at 96º directly into a four-foot by five-foot cedar-plank soaking pool. Even though this spring is a five-mile hike from the nearest road, there is no assurance of quiet privacy during the busy summer months, especially on weekends. There are no posted clothing requirements, which leaves it up to the mutual consent of those present.

Directions: From the town of Darrington, take FS 20 southeast approximately eight miles to the intersection with FS 23. Drive to the end of FS 23, which is the trailhead for Trail 643 up White Chuck Canyon. Consult with the Ranger Station in Darrington regarding weather and trail conditions before starting this trip.

Source map: *Mt. Baker-Snoqualmie National Forest*.

203   SCENIC HOT SPRINGS

● **East of the town of Skyhomish**

Wooden soaking box with a fabulous view located on a steep hillside above the Tye River in the Mt. Baker-Snoqualmie National Forest. Elevation 3,500 ft. Open all year.

Natural mineral water emerges from several springs at 108º and flows through a hose to a volunteer-built four-foot by six-foot soaking box. The temperature of the water in the pool can be controlled by diverting the inflow. The apparent local custom is clothing optional.

There are no services at the spring and it is 20 miles to all services in Skyhomish.

Directions: From Skyhomish on US 2 go ten miles east to the town of Scenic. Drive across the highway bridge spanning the Burlington-Northern Railrod tracks and watch for a primitive powerline road on your right, 0.2 mile east of milepost 59. Turn right and park as soon as possible. Walk east and start counting towers. Between the fourth and fifth towers there will be an unmarked path on the right, climbing steeply south up the hill to the springs. This is a rugged two-mile hike.

Source map: *Mt. Baker-Snoqualmie National Forest* (hot springs not shown on any map).

204   NOTARAS LODGE
242 Main St. E.   (509) 246-0462
■ Soap Lake, WA 98851   PR+MH

Large, new, western-style log-construction motel with in-room jet tubs and a public bathhouse. Open all year.

Natural mineral water is obtained from the city water system through an extra pipe which supplies Soap Lake water at temperatures up to 95º. Eight of the motel units are equipped with in-room jet tubs built for two. All rooms have an extra spigot over the bathtub to supply hot mineral water whenever desired. There is also a bathhouse building containing a sauna and two private-space, old-fashioned, single bathtubs supplied with mineral water. There is also a fresh water hydrojet pool maintained at 95-100º. The bathhouse facilities are available to the public as well as to registered guests.

Massage and motel rooms are available on the premises. All other services are within five blocks. Visa and MasterCard are accepted.

Location: On WA 17 in the town of Soap Lake.

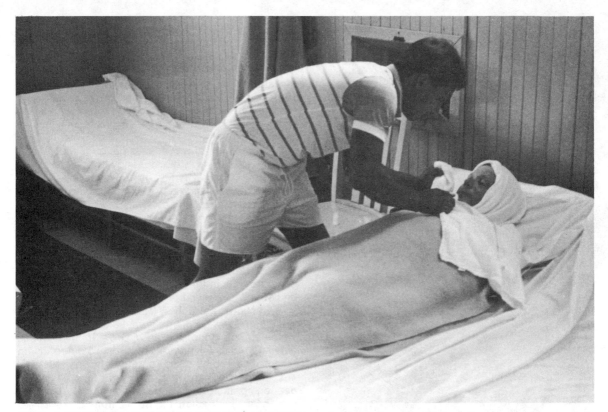

205　CARSON HOT SPRINGS RESORT

■
P.O. Box 370　　　　　(509) 427-8292
Carson, WA 98610　　　　PR+MH+CRV

Picturesque, historic resort which prides itself on having used "the same bath methods for over 100 years." Elevation 300 ft. Open all year.

Natural mineral water flows out of a spring at 126º and is piped to men's and women's bathhouses. There are eight claw-footed enamel tubs in the men's bathhouse, and nine in the women's. Temperature is controllable in each tub, which is drained and filled after each use, requiring no chemical treatment. An attendant, who is with you at all times, applies a sweat wrap after the soak. Bathing suits are not required in the bathhouses, which are available to the public as well as to registered guests.

Television, radio, newspapers and telephones are not available on the premises. Massage, restaurant, hotel rooms, cabins, overnight camping and RV hookups are available. A store and service station are within two miles. Hiking and fishing are nearby. Visa and MasterCard are accepted.

Directions: From the intersection of WA 14 and Bridge of the Gods over the Columbia River, go east on WA 14 and watch for signs. Phone for rates, reservations and further directions if necessary.

Carson Hot Springs Resort: This is one of the few locations which can claim to have delivered sweat wraps and mineral-water soaks in the same manner for 100 years.

St. Martins on the Wind: Part of the charm of this soaking pool is the sound of the river and a nearby waterfall.

206   ST. MARTINS ON THE WIND

● **On Carson H.S. Resort property   PR**

Small riverbank soaking pools 100 yards below a waterfall on the Wind River at the end of a sometimes difficult scramble over rocks and boulders. Elevation 150 ft. Open all year. Carson Hot Springs Resort charges a small fee for use of the pools.

Natural mineral water flows out of several seeps at 107º into three shallow sandy-bottom pools at the river's edge. Cooling is achieved by moving rocks to divert river water into a pool. The apparent local custom is clothing optional.

There are no services available on the premises, but overnight parking is not prohibited at the parking area. A restaurant, rooms and bathhouses are available within one mile at the Carson Hot Springs Resort. It is eight miles to campgrounds in the Gifford Pinchot National Forest and 15 miles to all other services in Hood River.

Directions: From the WA 14 highway bridge over the Wind River, go 3/4 mile east and turn north on a paved street signed *Berge Rd.* Drive 3/4 mile up this curving road to an intersection with two dirt roads on the left, marked by a sign on the right, *Indian Cabin Rd.* Take the hard left road 1/2 mile to a flat deadend parking area under a power line. A posted sign gives instruction for hiking from there to the springs and for paying the required fee.

207   WELLSPRING
Star Route   (206) 569-2514
☐   Ashford, WA 98304   PR

A charming, small, rustic spa located in the woods just outside the southwest entrance to Mt. Rainier National Park.

Private-space hot tubs are for rent to the public, using propane-heated spring water treated with chlorine. There are two cedar hot tubs, one in a lush forest setting overlooking a pond and one in a private Japanese garden. Water temperatures are maintained at 104-106º. Clothing is optional in private spaces.

Facilities include wood-fired cedar saunas and three cozy log cabins. Massage therapy is available on the premises. Visa and MasterCard are accepted. Phone for rates, reservations and directions.

▲ *Wellspring:* The tub may be filled with propane-heated spring water, but the natural surroundings make it feel almost as good as a real geothermal spring.

▲ *Town Tubs and Massage:* For busy city-dwellers the convenience of an in-town soaking tub makes up for natural scenery.

▲ *Fraternity Snoqualmie:* The pool may not contain mineral water, but the absence of swim suits is a plus to a skinnydipper.

208 TOWN TUBS AND MASSAGE

☐ 115 E. Olympia Ave.   (206) 943-2200
Olympia, WA 98501   PR

Modern rent-a-tub establishment in downtown Olympia, two blocks from Percival Landing on Puget Sound.

Private-space hot pools with cedar decks are for rent to the public, using gas-heated tap water treated with chlorine. There are six indoor acrylic pools with water temperature adjustable from 95-104º. Each unit has a personal sound system.

Therapeutic massage is available on the premises. Visa and MasterCard are accepted. Phone for rates, reservations and directions.

209 GRAND CENTRAL SAUNA & HOT TUB

☐ 32510 Pac. Hwy. So.   (206) 952-6154
Federal Way, WA 98003   PR

One of a chain of urban locations established by Grand Central, a pioneer in the private rent-a-tub business. Open all year.

Private-space hot pools using chlorine-treated tap water are for rent to the public by the hour. 19 indoor tubs are maintained at temperatures from 102-104º. Each unit contains a sauna.

No credit cards are accepted. Phone for rates, reservations and directions.

210 FRATERNITY SNOQUALMIE

☐ P.O. Box 748   (206) 392-NUDE
Issaquah, WA 98027   PR+CRV

Long-established nudist park occupying a hillside fruit orchard surrounded by evergreens. Elevation 500 ft. Open to members all year; open to guests from May through September.

The outdoor hydrojet pool is maintained at 104º all year. The outdoor swimming pool is solar heated, ranging from 80º in the summer to 50º in the winter. The wading pool is filled only in the summer. All pools use well water treated with chlorine. There is also a wood-fired sauna.

Clothing is not permitted in the pools or sauna.

Overnight camping and RV hookups are available on the premises. It is four miles to a cafe, store, service station and motel. Visa and MasterCard are accepted.

Note: This is a membership organization not open to the public for drop-in visits, but prospective members may be issued a guest pass by prior arrangement. Telephone or write for information and directions.

211 GOLDMYER HOTSPRINGS

202 N. 85th St. #106   (206) 789-5631
Seattle, WA 98103   PR+C

Very remote and beautiful mountain hot springs being preserved by a nonprofit volunteer organization. Prior reservations are required. (A $10 daily contribution is requested for each adult.) Elevation 1,800 ft. Open all year.

Natural mineral water flows into an old horizontal mine shaft at temperatures up to 120º. A dam has been built across the mouth of the shaft, creating a combination steam bath and soaking pool with water temperatures ranging up to 109º. The mineral water also falls into several nearby rock and cement soaking pools where the temperature is cooler in each lower pool. Clothing policy is determined by the caretaker based on the wishes of those present.

The springs are a 1/2 mile hike from the nearest parking, and overnight camping is available on the premises. It is 28 miles to all other services. Access roads vary in quality from Forest Service Class A to Class D, not suitable for trailers, motor homes and low-clearance vehicles. Ask for a current report on weather and road conditions when phoning for reservations and directions.

You can support the work of this organization by sending tax-deductible contributions to Goldmyer Hotsprings/Northwest Wilderness Programs, 202 N. 85th, #106, Seattle, WA 98103.

---

212 TUBS BELLEVUE

11023 N.E. 8th   (206) 462-TUBS
Bellevue, WA 98004   PR

Large, modern, pool-rental facility located in downtown Bellevue, a few miles east of Seattle.

Private-space hot pools are for rent to the public, using gas-heated tap water treated with chlorine. There are seventeen indoor acrylic pools with water temperature maintained at 102º. Each room also includes a dry sauna, music system, intercom and modern decor.

A juice bar is available on the premises. Visa, MasterCard and American Express are accepted. Phone for rates, reservations and directions. A membership at TUBS gains reservation privileges and discounts.

Goldmyer Hot Springs: The stairstep-falls arrangement makes it possible to start soaking in the hottest water and then move down to the cooler pools.

213 TUBS SEATTLE

4750 Roosevelt Way N.E. (206) 527-TUBS
☐ Seattle, WA 98105   PR

Large, modern, pool-rental facility located in the University district of Seattle.

Private, luxurious hot pools for rent to the public, using gas-heated tap water treated with chlorine. There are 12 indoor acrylic spas with water temperature maintained at 102-104º.

Each private suite also includes a dry heate sauna, stereo system, intercom, shower, and modern decor. An eleven-bed Sun Salon and a juice bar are also available. TUBS CLUB memberships gain members reservation privileges and discounts. Visa, MasterCard and American Express are accepted. Phone for rates and directions.

214 LAKE BRONSON CLUB

P.O. Box 1135   (206) 793-0286
☐ Sultan, WA 98294   PR+MH+CRV

Unusually spacious nudist park with its own 7 1/2-acre lake, waterfall and evergreen forest. Elevation 600 ft. Open all year.

One large, outdoor hydrojet pool using chlorine-treated artesian well water is maintained at 104º. The spring-fed lake warms to 80º in the summer and freezes over in the winter. There is also an electrically heated sauna. Clothing is prohibited in pool, sauna and lake and is optional elsewhere.

Rental trailers, laundry facilities, overnight camping and RV hookups are available on the premises. It is six miles to a cafe, store, service station and motel. No credit cards are accepted.

Note: This is a membership organization not open to the public for drop-in visits, but interested visitors may be issued a guest pass by prior arrangement. Telephone or write for information and directions.

Olympic Hot Springs: Some of the springs at this location are several degrees hotter than others. Wise visitors check water temperatures before plunging in.

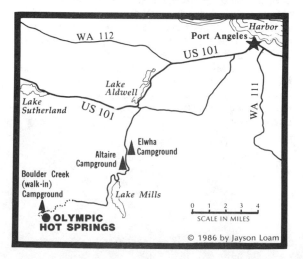

215   OLYMPIC HOT SPRINGS   (see map)

● **South of Port Angeles**

Several user-friendly, primitive springs surrounded by a lush rain forest at the end of an easy two-mile hike in Olympic National Park. Elevation 1,600 ft. Open all year.

Natural mineral water flows out of several springs at temperatures ranging from 100-112º. Volunteers have built a series of rock-and-sand soaking pools which permit the water to cool down to comfortable soaking temperatures. Official notices prohibiting nudity are posted often and promptly torn down, resulting in considerable uncertainty. Rangers have been observed issuing a citation after someone complained or after bathers didn't heed orders to dress. However, rangers have not made special trips to the area for the purpose of harassment.

Conscientious visitors have kept the area litter-free. Please do your part to maintain this standard.

There are no services on the premises, but there is a walk-in campground within 200 yards. It is eight miles to a cafe, store and service station, seven miles to a campground, and 20 miles to a motel and RV hookups.

Directions: From the city of Port Angeles, go ten miles west on US 101, turn south and follow signs to Elwha Valley. Continue south on paved road as it winds up Boulder Creek Canyon to where the road is closed due to slide damage. Park and walk the remaining two miles on the damaged paved road to the old end-of-road parking area. At the west end of that parking area is an unmarked, unmaintained path which crosses Boulder Creek and then leads into the hot-springs area. Most, but not all, paths indicate the presence of a nearby spring.

Source map: NPS *Olympic National Park* (hot springs not shown).

▲ This *Olympic Hot Springs* primitive pool has a good temperature for family fun.

▼ At the site of a long-gone lodge, the water in this larger pool is just right.

216 SOL DUC HOT SPRINGS RESORT

P.O. Box 2169   (206) 327-3583
Port Angeles, WA 98362   PR+MH+CRV

Extensively modernized, historic resort surrounded by the evergreen forest of Olympic National Park. Elevation 1,600 ft. Open mid-May through September. Pools are for day use only.

Natural mineral water flows out of a spring at 128° and is piped to a heat exchanger, where it heats the shower water and chlorine-treated creek water in the swimming pool. The cooled mineral water is then piped to three large outdoor soaking pools, which are maintained at 101-105° on a flow-through basis, requiring no chemical treatment of the water. These pools are equipped with access ramps for the convenience of handicapped persons. All pools are available to the public as well as to registered guests. The mineral water pools are open on weekends April through October. Bathing suits are required.

Locker rooms, a full-service restaurant, poolside deli bar, gift shop, cabins and RV hookups are available on the premises. It is 1/4 mile to a National Park campground and 15 miles to a service station. MasterCard, American Express, Discover and Visa are accepted.

Directions: From US 101, two miles west of Fairholm, take Soleduc River Road 12 miles south to resort.

Sol Duc Hot Springs Resort: In the 11 western states, these are the only commercial hot mineral water pools permitted in any National Park.

217 DOE BAY VILLAGE RESORT

Orcas Island Star Rt. 86   (206) 376-2291
Olga, WA 98279   PR+MH+CRV

Fantastic combination of running streams, waterfalls, and hot mineral water tubs outdoors on a deck with a spectacular view. Elevation sea level. Open all year.

Natural mineral water is pumped out of a well at 45°, is heated by electricity and piped to two outdoor pools, that are surrounded by trees and adjacent to a running stream with waterfalls. The pool water is continuously filtered, treated with bromine, and exchanged daily. Each pool is large enough for a dozen people, and one of them has hydrojets. Both are maintained at 101-104°, and a third pool contains cool water at air temperature. The wood-fired sauna is large enough for 20 people. The pools and sauna are available to the public as well as to registered guests. Bathing suits are optional.

Massage, vegetarian meals, rustic cabins, overnight camping, RV hookups and a hostel dormitory are available on the premises. Guided kayak trips and hikes in Moran State Park are nearby. It is seven miles to a store and service station. Visa, MasterCard and American Express are accepted.

Directions: Take the Anacortes Ferry to the San Juan Islands and get off at Orcas Island. Go north on Horseshoe Highway through Eastsound to the resort at the east end of island.

Doe Bay Village Resort: This hot-pool deck, overlooking Rosario Strait and the greenery of the San Juan Islands, gives the illusion of being up in a tree house.

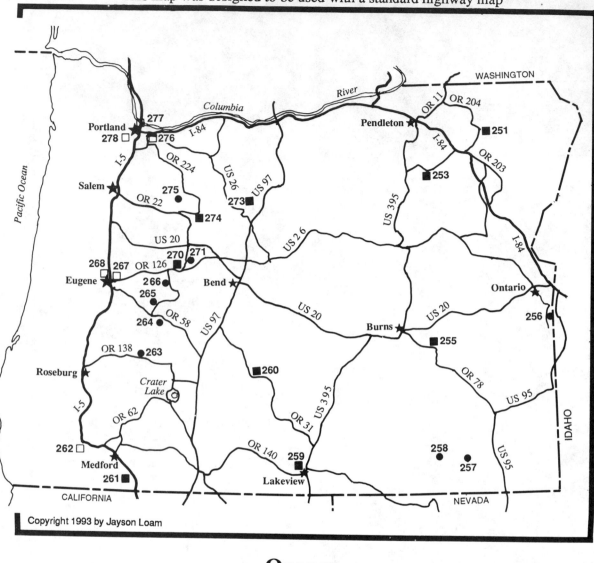

Oregon

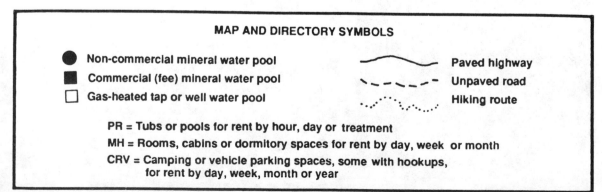

MAP AND DIRECTORY SYMBOLS

● Non-commercial mineral water pool

■ Commercial (fee) mineral water pool

□ Gas-heated tap or well water pool

~~~ Paved highway

- - - Unpaved road

⋯⋯ Hiking route

PR = Tubs or pools for rent by hour, day or treatment

MH = Rooms, cabins or dormitory spaces for rent by day, week or month

CRV = Camping or vehicle parking spaces, some with hookups, for rent by day, week, month or year

251   COVE SWIMMING POOL
907 Water St.   **(503) 568-4890**
■ **Cove, OR 97824**   **PR+CRV**

Large community swimming pool and picnic grounds in the foothills of the Wallowa Mountains. Elevation 3,200 ft. Open May 1 through Labor Day.

Natural mineral water at 86º flows up from a hot spring in the gravel bottom of the pool. Thanks to this continual flow-through, no chlorine is added. Bathing suits are required.

Picnic grounds, snack bar and overnight parking are available on the premises. It is two blocks to a cafe, store and service station, and 15 miles to a motel. No credit cards are accepted.

Directions: From I-84 in La Grandee, take OR 82 exit and go east to OR 237, then 14 miles south to the town of Cove.

▲ *Lehman Hot Springs:* Blessed with abundant hot mineral water and scenic property, new owners of this location have major expansion plans.

253   LEHMAN HOT SPRINGS
P.O. Box 263   **(503) 427-3015**
■ **Ukiah, OR 97880**   **PR+CRV**

Historic, major hot spring being developed into a large destination resort, surrounded by the beautiful Blue Mountain Forest. Elevation 4,300 ft. Open all year.

Natural mineral water flows out of several springs at temperatures up to 167º and is mixed with cold creek water before being piped to a series of outdoor pools. The first pool ranges from 112-115º, the second pool ranges from 107-110º, and the swimming pool ranges from 85-90º in the summer and from 90-96º in the winter. All pools operate on a flow-through basis so that a minimum of chlorination is necessary. The pools are available to the public as well as to registered guests. Bathing suits are required.

Lodging, dressing rooms, mineral water showers, snack bar, game room, RV hookups, camping and hiking trails are available on the premises. Fishing, hunting, cross country skiing and snowmobiling are available nearby. A store, service station and motel are within 18 miles. No credit cards are accepted.

Future development plans include an executive golf course, health spa, private therapy baths, hotel/restaurant and riding stables. Phone for status of construction.

Directions: From La Grande drive 8 miles west on I-84 to OR 244, then west for 35 miles and watch for Lehman Hot Springs signs.

◄ *Cove Swimming Pool:* This unique community plunge was built directly over the hot spring so it has a gravel bottom.

▲ Large indoor private-space soaking tubs are a popular part of the facilities available at *Crystal Crane Hot Springs*.

▲ *Crystal Crane Hot Springs:* Crowded city swimming pools do not permit inner tubes or other large inflated toys, but leisurely floats on an inner tube are part of the Crystal Crane experience.

---

255   **CRYSTAL CRANE HOT SPRINGS**
■   Route 1, Box 50-A   (503) 493-2312
    Burns, OR 97720

A growing health-oriented resort in the wide open spaces of eastern Oregon. Elevation 4200 ft. Open all year.

Natural mineral water flows out of several springs at 185º and supplies six private-space tubs which are maintained between 95-105º. The mineral water also fills a large, 80-foot pond. All the pools operate on a flow-through basis so that no chemical treatment of the water is necessary. Bathing suits are not required in the private-space pools.

Facilities include cabins, an organic greenhouse, and a camping area. Massage and vegetarian drinks are available on the premises. It is four miles to the nearest store and 24 miles to all other services in Burns. No credit cards are accepted.

Future plans include overnight facilities, RV hookups, a convention hall and a vegetarian restaurant. Call for status of construction.

Directions: From Burns, drive 24.5 miles east on OR 78 and watch for signs.

256   SNIVELY HOT SPRINGS

● **Southwest of the town of Owyhee**

Easily-accessible, primitive hot spring on the river's edge in the Owyhee River canyon. Elevation 2,400 ft. Open all year.

Natural mineral water flows out of several springs and a concrete standpipe at temperatures of more than 150º and then flows toward the river where volunteers have built several rock-and-sand soaking pools. The temperature in the pools is controlled by varying the amount of cold river water permitted to enter. The pools are visible from the road, so bathing suits are advisable.

There are no services available on the premises except for a large parking area on which overnight parking is not prohibited. It is ten miles to a cafe, store and service station, and 18 miles to a motel and RV hookups. Owyhee Lake,11 miles south of this hot spring, offers excellent fishing .

Directions: From the town of Owyhee, on OR 201, follow signs west toward Owyhee State Park. When the road enters Owyhee Canyon look for a large metal water pipe running up a steep slope on the west side of the road. 1.4 miles beyond that metal pipe, look on the other side of the road for a low concrete standpipe from which steaming water is flowing.

Source map: USGS *Owyhee Dam, Oregon.*

▲ *Snively Hot Springs:* This river-edge pool escapes spring washouts because the river is controlled by an upstream dam.

● Non-commercial mineral water pool

■ Commercial (fee) mineral water pool

□ Gas-heated tap or well water pool

 Paved highway

Unpaved road

Hiking route

PR = Tubs or pools for rent by hour, day or treatment

MH = Rooms, cabins or dormitory spaces for rent by day, week or month

CRV = Camping or vehicle parking spaces, some with hookups,
for rent by day, week, month or year

▲ *Whitehorse Ranch Hot Spring:* You can drive to this remote spring, but the unpaved road keeps traffic to a minimum.

257   WHITEHORSE RANCH HOT SPRING

● **Southeast of Alvord Desert**

A very remote, primitive hot spring requiring about 28 miles of unpaved-road travel in the dry, southeastern corner of Oregon.

Natural mineral water flows out of a spring at 114º and into a small, volunteer-built soaking pool which ranges in temperature from 104-112º. The overflow runs into a larger second pool which ranges in temperature from 70-90º, depending on air temperature and wind conditions. The apparent local custom is clothing optional.

There are no services on the premises, but there is plenty of level space on which overnight parking is not prohibited. It is 45 miles to all services.

Directions: From Burns Junction on US 95, go 21 miles south on US 95, then turn west on a gravel road and go 21 miles to Whitehorse Ranch. Cross a channel and pass by two roads which turn off to the left. At approximately five miles from the ranch, turn left on the third road which is marked by an orange flag on a power pole. Continue on that road for approximately three miles, curving around a butte. The spring is on the northwest side of the second butte.

Source map: BLM *Southern Malheur* (URA-MFP).

258   HART MOUNTAIN HOT SPRING
(see map)

●   **North of the town of Adel**

Semi-improved hot spring enclosed by a roofless, cement block wall and surrounded by miles of barren plateau within the Hart Mountain National Antelope Refuge. Elevation 6,000 ft. Open all year.

Natural mineral water flows out of a spring at 98º. The edge of the spring has been cemented to create a soaking pool which maintains that temperature. There is no posted clothing policy, which leaves it up to the mutual consent of those present.

There are no services available on the premises, but there is an abundance of level ground on which overnight parking is not prohibited. It is 20 miles to a cafe and store, and 40 miles to all other services.

Source map: *Hart Mountain National Antelope Refuge.*

▶ *Hart Mountain Hot Spring:* The cement block wall is to keep animals out, rather than to provide privacy for soakers.

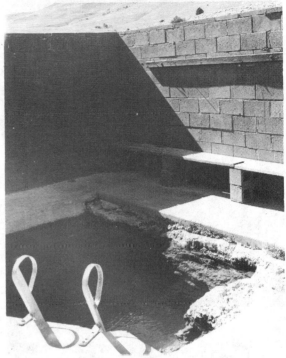

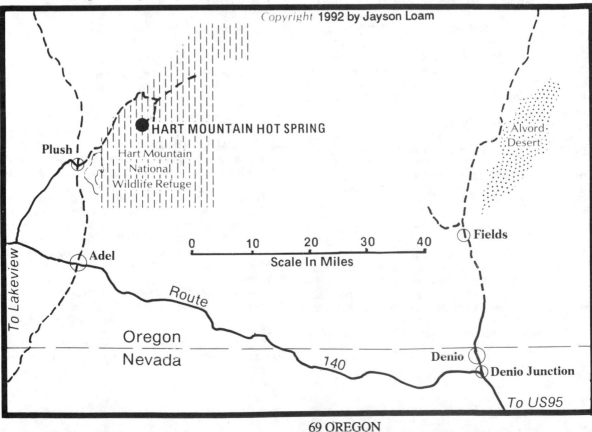

HART MOUNTAIN HOT SPRING

Alvord Desert

Plush

Hart Mountain National Wildlife Refuge

Fields

To Lakeview

Adel

0   10   20   30   40
Scale In Miles

Route

Oregon
Nevada

140

Denio
Denio Junction

To US95

Hunter's Hot Spring Resort: This geyser is hardly as large as Old Faithful, but it does erupt every two minutes.

259 HUNTER'S HOT SPRING RESORT

P.O. Box 1189   (503) 947-2127
Lakeview, OR 97630   PR+MH+CRV

Historic spa in the process of expansion and remodeling into a destination resort. Located in the rolling southern Oregon hills, two miles north of Lakeview. Elevation 4,200 ft. Open all year.

Natural mineral water flows out of several springs at temperatures up to 203º and into cooling ponds, from which it is piped to two outdoor pools and to a heat exchanger for the hot-water system in the buildings. Natural mineral water also erupts out of a geothermal geyser approximately every two minutes and flows into two large cooling ponds. The hydropool is maintained at 105º and the swimming pool is maintained at approximately 100º on a flow-through system with a minimum of chlorine treatment. Bathing suits are required.

A restaurant, store, service station, overnight camping and motel rooms are available on the premises. Pickup service to a private airport four miles away is also provided. Visa and MasterCard are accepted.

Location: Two miles north of the town of Lakeview on US 395.

Summer Lake Hot Springs: Chlorine treatment is not needed in this plunge which has continuous flow-through.

260 SUMMER LAKE HOT SPRINGS

(503) 943-3931
Paisley, OR 97636   PR+CRV

Small, indoor plunge in the wide open spaces south of Summer Lake. Elevation 4,200 ft. Open all year.

Natural mineral water flows out of a spring at 118º and cools as it is piped to the pool building. Water temperature in the indoor pool is maintained at 102º in the winter and 100º in the summer on a continuous flow-through basis that requires no chemical treatment of the water. Bathing suits are required.

Dressing rooms, overnight camping and RV hookups are available on the premises. It is six miles to all other services. No credit cards are accepted.

Location: Six miles northwest of the town of Paisley on OR 31. Watch for sign on north side of road.

261 JACKSON HOT SPRINGS

2253 Hwy 99 N.   (503) 482-3776
Ashland, OR 97520   PR+MH+CRV

Historic resort with public plunge, indoor soaking tubs, picnic grounds and RV park. Elevation 1,650 ft. Open all year. Swimming pool open May 1 to October 31.

Natural mineral water flows out of three springs at 96º-100º and directly into an outdoor swimming pool which is treated with chlorine and maintains a temperature of 84º-90º. There are three indoor individual soaking tubs large enough for two persons each, in which heated natural mineral water can be controlled up to 110º. These tubs are drained and cleaned after each use so that no chemical treatment of the water is necessary. Bathing suits are required, except in private rooms.

Dressing rooms, picnic grounds, cabins, overnight camping, RV hookups and a cafe are available on the premises. There is a store and service station within two blocks. Visa and MasterCard are accepted.

Location: Two miles north of Ashland at the Valley View Road exit from US 99.

Jackson Hot Springs: This pool and the private-space tubs are open to the public as well as to overnight customers.

Umpqua Warm Spring: Some rugged hot spring enthusiasts claim to enjoy the combination of a hot soak and cold rain in the face, but Oregon volunteers built a rustic shelter over this pool.

---

262   CEDAR CREST HOT TUB RENTALS
227 N.E. Hillcrest Drive   (503) 474-3090
☐   Grants Pass, OR 97526   PR

Clean and spacious rent-a-tub establishment located in north Grants Pass, near the K-Mart plaza.

Four fiberglass tubs, using gas-heated chlorine-treated tap water are for rent to the public by the hour. Water temperature in the tubs varies from 100°-104°. No credit cards are accepted.

Phone for rates, reservations and directions.

---

263   UMPQUA WARM SPRING (see map)

● **Northwest of Crater Lake**

Popular, small, semi-improved hot spring on a wooded bluff overlooking North Umpqua River. Located in the Umpqua National Forest at the end of a short new path. Elevation 2,600 ft. Open all year.

Natural mineral water flows out of a spring at 108° and directly into a sheltered, six-foot by six-foot pool which volunteers have carved out of the spring-built travertine deposit. There are no posted clothing requirements, and the location is quite remote, so a clothing-optional custom would be expected. However, the location is so popular, especially on summer weekends, that it is advisable to take a bathing suit with you. You may have to wait your turn to share a rather crowded pool.

There are no services available on the premises. It is three miles to a Forest Service campground and 25 miles to all other services.

Directions: Drive 60 miles east of Roseburg on OR 138 to Toketee Junction. Turn north on paved road FS 34 (Toketee Rigdon Road). Drive 2.3 miles, turn right on FS 3401 (Thorn Prairie Road) and drive two miles to the parking area. Walk across the new bridge over the North Umpqua River, bear right on the North Umpqua Trail and climb 1/4 mile east to springs.

Source map: *Umpqua National Forest.*

▲ Overlooking the North Umpqua River, and surrounded by green forest, *Umpqua Hot Springs* is a lovely setting.

▼ Unfortunately, *Umpqua Hot Springs* is so popular that the small pool fills up quickly, especially on weekends.

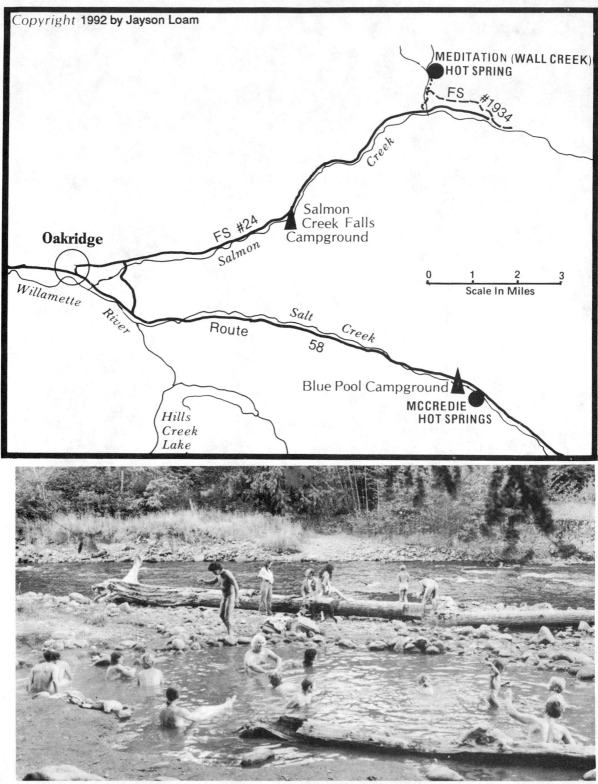

MEDITATION (WALL CREEK) HOT SPRING

FS #1934

Creek

Salmon Creek Falls Campground

FS #24

Oakridge

Salmon

Willamette

River

0   1   2   3
Scale In Miles

Route

Salt   Creek

58

Blue Pool Campground

MCCREDIE HOT SPRINGS

Hills Creek Lake

264   MCCREDIE HOT SPRINGS
(see map)

● **East of the town of Oakridge**

Easily-accessible, primitive hot springs with a strong skinny-dipping tradition, located on the north and south banks of Salt Creek in the Willamette National Forest. Elevation 2,100 ft. Open all year for day use only.

Natural mineral water flows out of several springs on the north bank at 120º, and on the south bank at 140º. The water is channeled into a series of shallow, volunteer-built, rock-and-mud pools where it cools as it flows toward the creek. Despite the proximity to a main highway, the apparent local custom is clothing optional.

There are no services available on the premises. There is a large level area nearby in which parking is permitted from sunrise to sunset only. It is less than one mile to a Forest Service campground and ten miles to all other services.

Directions: To reach the springs and pools on the north bank, drive from the town of Oakridge on OR 58, approximately ten miles east past Blue Pool Campground. At 1/10 mile past mile marker 45, turn right (south) into a large parking area between the road and the creek. Walk to the upstream (east) end of the parking area and follow a well-worn path 40 yards to the springs.

To reach the springs and soaking pools on the south bank, drive 1/2 mile east on OR 58, turn right on Shady Gap Road across the bridge and stay right on FS 5875. Drive 1/10 mile, park and look for an overgrown path that follows the creek 1/4 mile back downstream to the pools.

WARNING! Do not try to wade across Salt Creek to reach the south bank; the water is very deep and flows rapidly.

▲ *Meditation Pool Warm Spring:* The gentle tumbling sound of Wall Creek, a few feet away, is just enough for quiet centering.

265   MEDITATION POOL (WALL CREEK)
WARM SPRING   (see map)
● **Northeast of the town of Oakridge**

Idyllic, primitive warm spring on the wooded banks of Wall Creek at the end of a short, easy trail in the Willamette National Forest. Elevation 2,200 ft. Open all year, day use only.

Natural mineral water flows up through the gravel bottom of a volunteer-built, rock-and-sand pool at 104º. The pool temperature ranges up to 96º depending on air temperature and wind conditions. While the water is not hot enough for therapy soaking, it is ideal for effortless lolling. The apparent local custom is clothing optional.

There are no services available on the premises. It is five miles from the trailhead to a Forest Service campground and nine miles to all other services.

Directions: On OR 58 in the town of Oakridge at the "city center" highway sign, turn north on Rose St. over the train tracks. At First St., turn east and keep going as that street becomes FS 24. Approximately ten miles from Oakridge on FS 24, turn north on FS 1934 for 1/2 mile and watch for trailhead sign on west side of the road. There is no name or number given for the trail at the trailhead area. Follow a well-worn path along Wall Creek for 600 yards to the creekside pool. Source map: *Willamette National Forest.*

▲ *McCredie Hot Springs:* Families have found that the logs, cold creek-edge pools and
◄ shallow hot pools are great playgrounds.

266 TERWILLIGER (COUGAR) HOT SPRINGS (see map)
Southeast of the town of Blue River

A lovely series of user-friendly, log-and-stone soaking pools in a picturesque, forest canyon at the end of an easy one-quarter-mile trail in the Willamette National Forest. Elevation 3,000 ft. Open all year for day use only..

Natural mineral water flows out of a spring at 116º and directly into the first of a series of volunteer-built pools, each of which is a few degrees cooler than the one above. An organized group of volunteers has also built access steps and railings. The apparent local custom is clothing optional.

There are no services available on the premises. There is a walk-in campground within one-half mile. Overnight parking is prohibited along the road for one mile on both sides of the trailhead. It is four miles to a Forest Service campground and eight miles to all other services.

Directions: From OR 126 approximately five miles east of Blue River, turn south on FS 19 along the west side of Cougar Reservoir. The marked hot-springs trailhead is on the west side of the road just past milepost 7 and 0.3 mile south of Boone Creek. A large parking area is on the east side of the road, 0.1 mile beyond the trailhead. Parking is permitted from sunrise to sunset only.

Reference map: *Willamette National Forest* (hot springs not shown).

▲ Fallen logs at *Terwilliger Hot Springs* are part of the primitive forest setting.

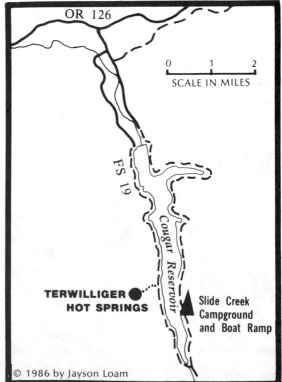

© 1986 by Jayson Loam

267 SPRINGFIELD SPAS

1100 Main St.   (503) 741-1777
Springfield, OR 97477   PR

Well-maintained, suburban, rent-a-tub establishment located on the main street.

Private-space hydrojet pools using chlorine-treated tap water are for rent to the public by the hour. Twelve fiberglass tubs in open-roof enclosed spaces are maintained at 102º. Each unit includes a covered dressing area with shower and stereo.

Three tanning beds are available on the premises. Visa, MasterCard and Discover are accepted. Phone for rates, reservations and directions.

268 ONSEN HOT TUB RENTALS

1883 Garden Ave.   (503) 345-9048
Eugene, OR 97403   PR

Well-maintained, enclosed-pool, rent-a-tub establishment located near the University of Oregon.

Private-space hydrojet pools using chlorine-treated tap water are for rent to the public by the hour. Fourteen fiberglass tubs in open-roof enclosed spaces are maintained at 102º. Each unit includes a covered dressing area.

No credit cards are accepted. Phone for rates, reservations and directions.

▲ *Onsen Hot Tub Rentals:* At least sunshine, fresh air and the stars at night are available in roofless enclosures.

▲ *Springfield Spas:* The walls around most urban rental tubs, such as this one, provide total privacy but no scenery.

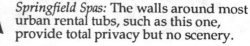

270 BELKNAP LODGE & HOT SPRINGS

P.O. Box 1   (503) 822-3512
Belknap Springs, OR 97413   MH+CRV

Attractive, riverside resort in a wilderness setting with in-room jettubs, campground and RV park, surrounded by the lush greenery of Willamette National Forest. Elevation 1,700 ft. Open all year.

Natural mineral water flows out of a spring at 196º and is piped into a combination reservoir and heat exchanger where heat is extracted for space heating and for the hot water supply in the lodge and the RV park. The cooled mineral water is piped to outdoor pools at the lodge and the RV park. Both pools are lightly treated with chlorine and maintained at a temperature of 104º in the winter and 100º in the summer. Six lodge rooms have indoor hydrojet tubs controllable up to 110º. These tubs are drained and cleaned after each use so that no chemical treatment of the water is needed. The use of the pools is limited to registered guests. Bathing suits are required, except in private rooms.

Rooms, overnight camping, RV hookups, fishing and white water rafting are available on the premises. It is six miles to all other services. Visa and MasterCard are accepted.

Location: On OR 126, 6 miles east of the town of McKenzie Bridge. Follow signs.

Belknap Hot Springs: A tiled swimming pool, in its own enclosure, is provided for registered guests in the RV park.

Hot mineral water flows through the pipe suspended over the river near the lodge pool and then into the ingenious heat exchanger tank at the end of the pool.

271   BIGELOW HOT SPRING

● **Northeast of the town of McKenzie Bridge**

A small, rock-and-sand pool in a fern-lined grotto on the McKenzie River. Elevation 2,000 ft. Open all year.

A small flow of natural mineral water (130º) bubbles up from the bottom of a volunteer-dug pool, maintaining a comfortable 102º to 104º soaking temperature. The apparent local custom is clothing optional.

There are no services available on the premises. It is 1 1/2 miles to a campground (Ollalie), three miles to a motel and RV hookups (Belknap Hot Springs), and six miles to all other services.

Directions: From the town of McKenzie Bridge, drive nine miles northeast on OR 126. Drive 4/10 mile past milepost 15, then turn left onto FS 2654 (Deer Creek Road). Park just beyond the bridge over the McKenzie River. Follow the signed McKenzie River Trail a short way south and watch for the second faint path heading down the steep bank to the pool at the river's edge.

▲ *Bigelow Hot Spring:* This primitive pool cannot be seen from the road 100 feet away so skinnydipping is practical.

▲ *Kah-Nee-Tah Vacation Resort Village*: Bear sculptures decorate the large pools.

◄ Rental tepees are full size family accommodations, not child play toys.

273   KAH-NEE-TA VACATION RESORT VILLAGE

P.O. Box K   **(503) 553-1112**
■ **Warm Springs, OR 97761   PR+MH+CRV**

A modern resort owned and operated by the Confederated Tribes of the Warm Springs Indian Reservation. In these foothills on the east side of the Cascade Mountains, the sun shines 300 days a year. Elevation 1,500 ft. Open all year.

Natural mineral water flows out of a spring at 140º and is piped to the bathhouse and swimming pool. The large outdoor swimming pool is chlorinated and maintained at a temperature of 95º. The men's and women's bathhouses each contain five tiled Roman tubs in which the soaking temperature is individually controlled up to 110º. Tubs are drained and filled after each use. Pools and bathhouses are available to the public as well as to registered guests. Bathing suits are required in public areas.

Massage, dressing rooms, restaurant, cabins, teepees, overnight camping, RV hookups and miniature golf are available on the premises. A resort hotel and golf course are also located on the property. It is 11 miles to a store and service station. Visa, MasterCard, American Express, Diner's Club and Carte Blanche are accepted.

Directions: From US 26 in Warm Springs, follow signs 11 miles northeast to resort.

▲ The tepee portion of the campground at *Kah-Nee-Tah* is located conveniently close to the bathhouse and pool area.

▼ On this Indian reservation, squishy-bottom primitive soaking pools have been replaced with tiled fiberglass pools.

◄ Water filtration, hydrojets and a variety of soaking pool temperatures are designed to meet the needs of modern vacationers.

Breitenbush Hot Springs: Quiet meditation is encouraged in this soaking pool, which enjoys a view of the Breitenbush River.

The holistic community which operates *Breitenbush Hot Springs* sponsors groups such as this Summer Solstice Gathering.

274 BREITENBUSH HOT SPRINGS RETREAT AND CONFERENCE CENTER

P.O. Box 578   (503) 854-3314
Detroit, OR 97342   PR+MH

A rustic, older resort that has been renovated by the intentional community that operates the retreat center as a worker-owned cooperative. It is located on the banks of the Breitenbush River, surrounded by the Willamette National Forest. Elevation 2,300 ft. Open all year.

Natural mineral water flows out of springs and artesian wells at temperatures up to 180º. There are four outdoor soaking pools using flow-through mineral water requiring no chemical treatment. Each pool is maintained at a different temperature, ranging from 60º-111º. There are three outdoor pools in the meadow which operate on a flow-through basis with temperatures averaging between 100-110º, depending on weather conditions. The sauna/steambath building is supplied with 180º water direct from an adjoining well and spring. The pools are available to the public for day use as well as to overnight guests, but prior reservations are advised. Clothing is optional in the tubs and sauna area, unless a workshop leader requests special swimsuit-required times.

Massage, hydrotherapy, aromatherapy and metaphysical counseling (by reservation), vegetarian meals and cabins are available on the premises. Daily Well Being Programs are offered without charge.

It is 11 miles to a store, service station and phone, 1 1/2 miles to overnight camping and 70 miles to RV hookups. Organizations and individuals are invited to request rates for facilities suitable for seminars and conferences. Visa and MasterCard are accepted.

Location: 11 miles northeast of Detroit. Phone for rates, reservations and directions.

MAP AND DIRECTORY SYMBOLS

● Non-commercial mineral water pool
■ Commercial (fee) mineral water pool
□ Gas-heated tap or well water pool

〜〜〜 Paved highway
〜 〜 〜 Unpaved road
∴∴∴ Hiking route

PR = Tubs or pools for rent by hour, day or treatment
MH = Rooms, cabins or dormitory spaces for rent by day, week or month
CRV = Camping or vehicle parking spaces, some with hookups,
            for rent by day, week, month or year

This cluster of *Breitenbush Hot Springs* pools was designed to have symbolic significance as well as to provide a variety of water temperatures.

▲ *Bagby Hot Springs:* One-piece soaking tubs hewn from huge logs are the primary furnishings in the communal bathhouse.

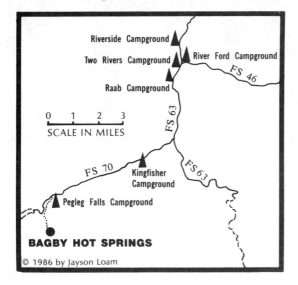

Riverside Campground ▲

Two Rivers Campground ▲ ▲ River Ford Campground

FS 46

Raab Campground ▲

FS 63

0   1   2   3
SCALE IN MILES

FS 70   FS 63

Kingfisher Campground ▲

▲ Pegleg Falls Campground

BAGBY HOT SPRINGS

© 1986 by Jayson Loam

▲ At all of the *Bagby Hot Springs* tubs admission of more hot mineral water is controlled by removable flume plugs.

275 BAGBY HOT SPRINGS

(see map)

● **Southeast of the town of Estacada**

One of the best. A well-planned rustic facility featuring hot mineral water supplied through a 150-foot log flume. A lush rain forest and tumbling mountain stream make the 1 1/2 mile access trail enjoyable in its own right. Elevation 2,200 ft. Open all year.

Natural mineral water emerges from two springs at 135º, and is flumed to an outdoor round cedar tub on a deck at the upper spring site and to two bathhouse buildings at the lower spring site. The partially-roofed bathhouse is a replica of the one that burned down in 1979, offering five hand-hewn cedar tubs in private rooms. The open-sided bathhouse offers a single communal space containing three hewn tubs and a round cedar tub. A flume diversion gate at each tub brings in more hot water whenever desired, and all tubs are drained and cleaned daily, so no chemical treatment of the water is necessary. There are no posted clothing requirements, and the apparent local custom in the communal bathhouse is clothing-optional.

All facilities are made possible and are managed by the Friends of Bagby Hot Springs, Inc., a non-profit volunteer organization operating under a special use permit with the Forest Service to restore, preserve and maintain the area. Volunteers also serve as hosts for the public. You can support this pioneering organization by sending tax-deductible contributions to Friends of Bagby, Inc., P.O. Box 15116, Portland, OR 97215.

There is a picnic area on the premises, but no overnight camping is permitted. A walk-in campground is located at Shower Creek, 1/3 mile on the trail beyond Bagby. A drive-in Forest Service Campground (Nohorn) is located adjacent to the trailhead parking area and the Pegleg Falls Campground is located 1/2 mile northeast of the trailhead. All other services are available 32 miles away in Estacada.

276 FOUR SEASONS HOT TUBBING

19059 S.E. Division   (503) 666-3411
☐ Gresham, OR 97030   PR

Attractive, suburban rent-a-tub facility featuring enclosed outdoor tubs. Open all year.

Private-space hot pools using chlorine-treated tap water are for rent to the public by the hour. Six enclosed, outdoor fiberglass hydrojet pools are maintained at a temperature of 104º. Each unit includes indoor dressing room, shower and toilet.

Visa and MasterCard are accepted. Phone for rates, reservations and directions.

277A OPEN AIR HOT TUBBING

11126 N.E. Halsey   (503) 257-8191
☐ Portland, OR 97220   PR

Unique, suburban rent-a-tub featuring open-roofed wood patios. Open all year.

Private-space hot pools using chlorine-treated tap water are for rent to the public by the hour. Six enclosed, outdoor fiberglass hydrojet pools are maintained at temperatures ranging from 102-104º. Each unit has an outdoor water spray over the pool and an indoor dressing room with shower and toilet. Three of the units can be combined to accommodate a party of 24. There is a sauna in one unit.

An open-air tanning salon is available on the premises. Visa and MasterCard are accepted. Phone for rates, reservations and directions.

277B INNER CITY HOT SPRINGS

2927 N.E. Everett   (503) 238-4010
☐ Portland, OR 97232   PR

Open-air, family-style pools and sauna in a garden setting near downtown Portland.

Two communal hydrojet pools, cold pool, sauna and sundeck are for rent to the public by the hour. Both hot pools use gas-heated tap water treated with chlorine and are maintained at 104º. Bathing suits are optional in the pool and sauna areas.

Massage, chiropractic care, homeopothy, rebirthing and accupressure are available on the premises. No credit cards are accepted. Phone for rates, reservations and directions.

278 ELITE TUBBING AND TANNING

4240 S.W. 10th   (503) 641-7727
☐ Beaverton, OR 97005   PR

Private rent-a-tub suites in a remodeled house across from Beaverton's Montgomery Ward store. Open all year.

Private-space hot pools using chlorine-treated tap water are for rent to the public by the hour. Six indoor fiberglass hydrojet pools are maintained at a temperature of 103º. Each suite includes a shower and toilet.

Facilities include tanning equipment. Massage is available on the premises. Visa and MasterCard are accepted. Phone for rates, reservations and directions.

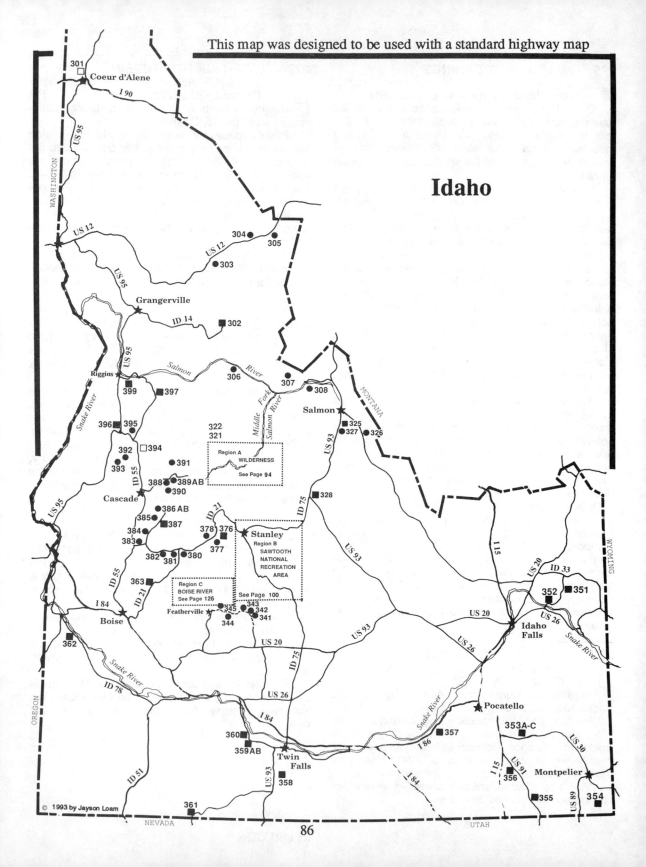

Idaho

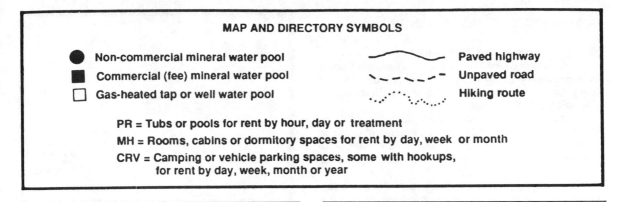

MAP AND DIRECTORY SYMBOLS

● Non-commercial mineral water pool

■ Commercial (fee) mineral water pool

☐ Gas-heated tap or well water pool

〜〜〜 Paved highway

- - - - - Unpaved road

····· Hiking route

PR = Tubs or pools for rent by hour, day or treatment

MH = Rooms, cabins or dormitory spaces for rent by day, week or month

CRV = Camping or vehicle parking spaces, some with hookups,
for rent by day, week, month or year

---

301   BENNETT BAY INN
☐   E 5144 I-90   (208) 664-6168
       Coeur D'Alene, ID 83814   PR+MH

Modern motel with hot-pool theme suites, store and boat dock on Lake Coeur D'Alene, three miles from the town of Coeur D'Alene and 30 miles from Spokane, Washington.

Pools in motel suites are for rent to the public by the hour and by the day. Lake water is heated by electricity, treated with chlorine, and maintained at 102º. There are six indoor, fiberglass pools, five of them in spectacular theme rooms. Movies are available - all ratings. The outdoor swimming pool is filled with unheated lake water and treated with chlorine.

Facilities include free rowboat use with room rental. Visa, MasterCard, American Express and Diners Club are accepted. Phone for rates, reservations and directions.

302   RED RIVER HOT SPRINGS
■   Red River Road   (208) 983-2800
       Elk City, ID 83525   PR+MH+CRV

Friendly, remote, rustic resort featuring both public and private-space pools, surrounded by the tall timber in the Nezperce National Forest. Elevation 5,200 feet. Open all year.

Natural mineral water flows out of ten springs at temperatures up to 130º. The chlorine-treated swimming pool temperature varies from 88º in the summer to 72º in the winter. The outdoor flow-through soaking pool is maintained at 104º and requires no chemical treatment. There are also three claw-footed bathtubs located in private spaces. These are drained and cleaned after each use. In a fourth private space, there is an authentic galvanized horse trough which is surprisingly comfortable for a two-person soak. Pools are available to the public as well as to registered guests. Bathing suits are required in public areas.

Dressing rooms, a cafe, store, rustic cabins, and overnight camping are available on the premises. Hiking, fishing, cross-country skiing, snowmobiling, and horse trails are nearby. It is 30 miles to a service station and 150 miles to RV hookups. No credit cards are accepted. Future plans include modern cabins and a complete RV park. Phone ahead for the status of construction.

Directions: From the town of Grangeville, take ID 14 to Elk City, then go 25 miles east to the resort. The last 11 miles are on an easy gravel road.

◄   *Red River Hot Springs:* Thanks to abundant mineral water, this flow-through soaking pool does not need chlorine treatment.

303 STANLEY HOT SPRINGS

● **Northeast of the town of Lowell**

A series of delightful rock and log soaking pools in Huckleberry Creek canyon at the end of a rugged five-mile trail in the Selway-Bitterroot Wilderness. Elevation 3,600 ft. Open all year.

Natural mineral water flows out of a canyon-bank at 110º and cools as it tumbles through a series of volunteer-built pools which range in temperature from 90-110º. The apparent local custom is clothing optional.

There are no services available on the premises but there are spacious campsites tucked into the nearby woods. There is a drive-in Forest Service campground at the trailhead. All other services are in Lowell, 26 miles from the trailhead.

Directions: On US 12, drive 26 miles northeast of Lowell to the Wilderness Gateway Compound (ranger station and visitor center). Go past Loops A and B, and the amphitheater, to Trail 211 parking area. Hike 5 miles east on Trail 211, then 1/2 mile south on FS 221 to the springs.

Source maps: *USGS Huckleberry Butte; Clearwater National Forest.*

---

304 WEIR CREEK HOT SPRINGS

● **Northeast of the town of Lowell**

Secluded, primitive hot springs and creekside soaking pool reached via a sometimes difficult half-mile path in Clearwater National Forest. Elevation 2,900 ft. Open all year.

Natural mineral water flows out of several springs at 117º and is channeled through a wooden gutter to a volunteer-built pool lined with split logs. Temperature can be controlled by moving the gutter to add or divert the flow of hot water. The apparent local custom is clothing optional.

There are no services available on the premises. It is eight miles to a Forest Service campground, 16 miles to a restaurant and motel, and 35 miles to all other services.

Directions: From Lowell, drive 45 miles northeast on US 12 to mile marker 142. Park in pullout area just east of that mile marker at a bridge spanning Weir Creek. Follow an unmarked, unmaintained path up the west side of the creek for slightly less than 1/2 mile to the springs. Wherever it appears that the path divides, stay with the fork that keeps the creek in sight.

Source map: *Clearwater National Forest.*

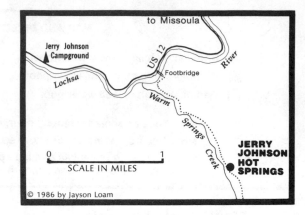

© 1986 by Jayson Loam

305 JERRY JOHNSON HOT SPRINGS
(see map)

● **Southwest of the town of Missoula**

Delightful group of user-friendly, primitive hot springs at the end of an easy, one-mile hike through a beautiful forest along the east bank of Warm Springs Creek. Elevation 3,200 ft. Open all year, day use only.

Odorless natural mineral water flows out of many fissures in the creek bank at 114º and also out of several other springs at temperatures up to 110º. Volunteers have constructed rock-and-mud soaking pools along the edge of the river and near the springs. The temperature within each pool is controlled by admitting cold creek water as needed or by diverting the hotter flow to let a pool cool down. The apparent local custom is clothing optional.

There are no services on the premises. However, there are three uncrowded Forest Service campgrounds within five miles of the Jerry Johnson Hot Springs trailhead. It is ten miles to a cafe, service station and all other services.

Directions: Drive on US 12 to Warm Springs Park bridge trailhead, which is located 1/2 mile west of mile marker 152. Park in large area on north side of US 12, walk over bridge and follow FS 49 one mile southeast to springs.

Source map: *Clearwater National Forest.*

► *Jerry Johnson Hot Springs:* This natural-bottom upper pool contains 105º water and overlooks a lovely green meadow. (More photographs on the next page.)

89 IDAHO

▲ Volunteer-built creekside soaking pools have to be rebuilt from scratch each year after being washed out by spring run-off.

▼ The trail to *Jerry Johnson Hot Springs* starts at this bridge, which is across the highway from the parking area.

▲
▼ At *Jerry Johnson Hot Springs*, geothermal water flows from the ground in many places, resulting in a wide variety of volunteer-built soaking pools.

---

306   BARTH HOT SPRINGS

● **West of the town of North Fork**

A truly unexpected, claw-footed bathtub in a remote section of the main Salmon River known as the *River of No Return*. Elevation 2,700 ft. Open all year. but access is extremely difficult in the winter becaue the Salmon River freezes over.

Natural mineral water flows out of many small seeps at temperatures up to 140º and cools as it is gathered into a PVC pipe carrying it to the outdoor bathtub. River guides have also constructed a rock and sand soaking pool. There are no posted clothing requirements, which leaves that matter up to the mutual consent of those present.

There are no services available on the premises, nor are there any roads to this area. Access is by raft or jet boat. It is 22 miles to the nearest road and 65 miles to all services.

Source maps: Forest Service, *The Salmon, River of No Return.*

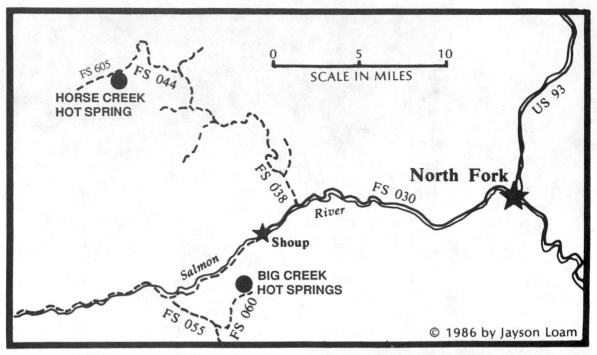

FS 605
FS 044
**HORSE CREEK
HOT SPRING**

0   5   10
SCALE IN MILES

US 93

FS 038

North Fork

FS 030

River

Shoup

Salmon

**BIG CREEK
HOT SPRINGS**

FS 055
FS 060

© 1986 by Jayson Loam

Horse Creek Hot Spring: The small soaking pool and nearby campground are on the edge of a beautiful alpine valley.

The enclosure does provide privacy, but it also makes it impossible to enjoy a soak and the view at the same time.

---

307   HORSE CREEK HOT SPRING
(see map)

● **Northwest of the town of North Fork**

Rock-lined, primitive hot spring enclosed by four walls in a very remote section of beautiful Salmon National Forest. Elevation 6,200 ft. Open all year.

Natural mineral water flows out of a spring at 97º and directly into the pool, which is surrounded by a roofless bathhouse. The apparent local custom is clothing optional.

There is a picnic area with table and rest rooms available at the springs. It is one mile to a campground and 35 miles to all other services.

Directions: From the town of North Fork, go west on FS 030, north on FS 038, west and north on FS 044, then west and south on FS 065 to the spring.

Source map: *Salmon National Forest.*

▲
▼ *Big Creek Hot Springs:* There is no enclosure around this large, temperature-controllable pond, and we thank the volunteers who built it and signed it.

308   BIG CREEK HOT SPRINGS
(see map)

● **West of the town of North Fork**

Large waist-deep pool fed by dozens of geothermal outflows along Warm Springs Creek in a remote, rocky canyon in Salmon National Forest. Elevation 4,800 ft. Open all year.

Natural mineral water emerges from a rocky hillside at 185º and flows toward the rock and cement pool built by the Sterlings in 1987, and through other small pools in the creekbed. Cold water is scarce, so pool temperatures must be controlled by diverting the hot water flow as needed. There are no services available on the premises. It is 33 miles to all services.

Source maps: *Salmon National Forest*; USGS *Shoup, Idaho-Montana.*

This is the region in which to totally escape urban noise pollution, because the only way to reach these springs is to hike or float in on a raft, or both. It is possible to plan a rugged backpack route which will take you to several springs over a two or three day period. It is equally possible to find packaged river-raft trips, featuring hot springs, which fly you to an upriver air strip, carry all your food and gear, cook all your meals and even wash the dishes, while you sit back and enjoy unsurpassed beauty. For information on raft trip charters, contact River Odysseys West, P.O. Box 579, Coeur d'Alene, ID 83814. (800) 451-6034.

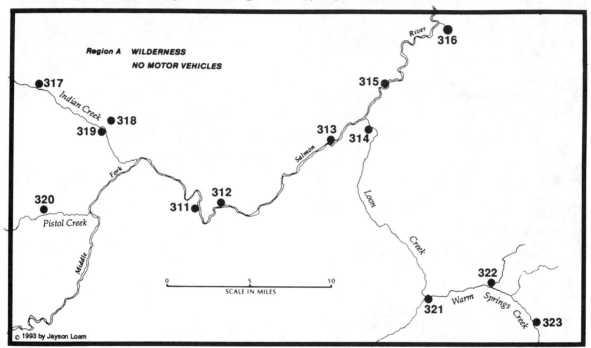

Region A WILDERNESS
NO MOTOR VEHICLES

SCALE IN MILES

© 1993 by Jayson Loam

WILDERNESS HOT SPRINGS ACCESSIBLE BY RAFT

311   SUNFLOWER FLATS HOT SPRINGS

Natural mineral water from a group of hot springs (109º) flows through some shallow, cliff-top pools before dropping to the river's edge in the form of a hot waterfall.

Sunflower Flats Hot Springs: River rafts can beach within a few feet of this hot waterfall. Volunteers have also built soaking pools near the source springs.

▲ *Hood Ranch Hot Springs:* Even in a wilderness area it is sometimes necessary to use some galvanized iron pipe.

◄ *Whitey Cox Hot Springs:* Except for its remoteness, this soaking pool comes very close to meeting the ideal image.

---

312   HOOD RANCH HOT SPRINGS

●

The geothermal water from springs with temperatures up to 149º cools as it flows through pipes to a crude shower-bath and soaking pool within 100 yards of the river.

---

313   WHITEY COX HOT SPRINGS

●

A beautiful riverside meadow contains several classic, natural soaking pools supplied from nearby hot springs (131º) through channels where the water cools on the way.

Lower Loon Creek Hot Springs: Some hardy individuals trot back and forth between this hot pool and the nearby cold creek.

314   LOWER LOON CREEK HOT SPRINGS

●

A large, log soaking pool on the edge of Loon Creek is supplied by several springs with temperatures up to 120º. This pool does require a 1/4-mile hike from the raft-landing beach where the creek joins the river.

315   HOSPITAL BAR HOT SPRINGS

●

Dozens of fissures in the riverbank rocks emit 115º geothermal water which is collected for soaking in a few shallow pools next to a favorite landing spot for rafts.

316   COLD SPRINGS CREEK HOT SPRING

●

Located a mile from the river, this spring emits 140º mineral water which flows first into a cooling pond and then is piped to this cozy soaking box.

Hospital Bar Hot Springs: At this geothermal stop it is possible to step directly from a raft into a hot pool.

Cold Creek Hot Springs: Energetic joggers like the challenege of a one mile uphill run ending in this soothing hot pool.

WILDERNESS HOT SPRINGS ACCESSIBLE BY TRAIL ONLY

317 KWIS KWIS HOT SPRINGS

Outflow temperature - 156º

318 MIDDLE FORK INDIAN CREEK HOT SPRINGS

Outflow temperature› 162º.

319 INDIAN CREEK HOT SPRINGS

Outflow temperature› 190º.

320 PISTOL CREEK HOT SPRINGS

Outflow temperature› 115º.

321 OWEN CABIN HOT SPRINGS

Outflow temperature› 133º.

322 FOSTER RANCH HOT SPRINGS

Outflow temperature› 135º.

323 SHOWER BATH HOT SPRINGS

Outflow temperature› 122º.

For trail information see *The Hiker's Guide to Hot Springs in the Pacific Northwest* by Evie Litton.
Available for $9.95 + $2.50 shipping from Falcon Press
P.O. Box 1718, Helena, MT 59624. (800) 582-2665.

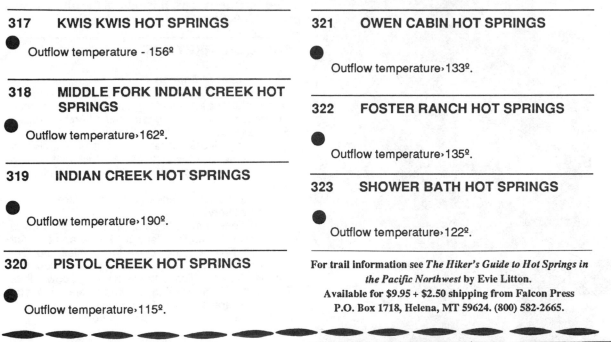

► *Salmon Hot Spring:* Closed for several decades, this turn-of-the-century pool is once more available to the public.

325 SALMON HOT SPRING

P.O. Box 1067	(208) 756-4449
Salmon, ID 83467	PR+CRV

Rustic rural plunge with a colorful past, undergoing major renovation. Elevation 4,950 feet. Open all year.

Natural mineral water flows abundantly out of a spring at 115º and is piped to a large swimming pool which is maintained at 98º to 102º. The flow-through pool is drained and refilled nightly, so no chemical treatment of the water is needed. Bathing suits are required.

Dressing rooms and primitive camping are available on the premises. It is eight miles to all other services. Visa and MasterCard are accepted.

Directions: From Salmon, drive four miles south on US93, turn left on Airport Road and drive .8 mile to "T" intersection. Turn left again and follow Warm Springs Creek Road 3.5 miles to the spring.

Sharkey Hot Spring: Compared to large modern spas, this relic is the ultimate in functional no-frills construction.

326 SHARKEY HOT SPRING

● **East of Salmon**

A cozy wooden soaking box is all that remains of an old sheepherder's bathhouse in an open sagebrush canyon above the Lemhi Valley. Elevation 5,300 feet. Open all year.

Natural mineral water flows out of a spring at 105º directly into the four foot by four foot by two foot box. The apparent local custom is clothing optional.

There are no services on the premises. It is 23 miles to all services.

Directions: From Salmon, drive east on ID28 to the Tendoy store. Turn left, go .2 mile and turn left again on Tendoy Lane. Drive three miles and turn right onto Warm Springs Wood Road. Follow this dirt road for two miles to the high voltage power line. Park just before crossing the bridge and walk 100 yards up a grassy trail to the spring.

Source map: *Salmon National Forest.*

Goldbug Hot Springs: The strenuous two-mile climb and the mile-high altitude keep most tourists away from this spectacular site.

327 GOLDBUG HOT SPRINGS

● **Southwest of the town of Salmon**

Many delightful pools and cascades of various temperatures at the end of a steep, two-mile trail up a beautiful canyon in Salmon National Forest. Elevation 5,200 feet. Open all year.

Natural mineral water flows out of several springs at temperatures up to 110º and combines with cold creek water as it tumbles down the canyon. Volunteers have added rock-and-sand dams to deepen the water-worn cascade pools. Temperatures in these cascade pools are determined by the rate of cold water runoff. Some of the pools offer a sepectacular view down the canyon. The apparent local custom is clothing optional.

There are no services available on the premises. Parking is available at the trailhead, and it is one mile to other services in Elk Bend.

Directions: On US 93 approximately 23 miles south of Salmon, look for mile marker 282. Go east on a short gravel road to the trailhead parking area. This parking lot is adjacent to private property. Cross the footbridge over Warm Springs Creek and follow the often steep trail up the canyon to the springs near the top of the ridge.

328 CHALLIS HOT SPRINGS

H/C 63 Box 1779 (208) 879-4442
Challis, ID 83226 PR+CRV

Historic community plunge and campground on the banks of the Salmon River. Elevation 5,000 ft. Pools open all year; campground open April 1 to November.

Natural mineral water flows from several springs at temperatures up to 127º and is piped to flow-through indoor and outdoor pools which require no chemical treatment. The temperature of the outdoor pool is maintained at approximately 90º, and the temperature of the indoor pool ranges from 108-110º. Bathing suits are required.

Changing rooms, picnic areas, camping and RV hookups are available on the premises. All other services are available within seven miles. Visa and MasterCard are accepted.

Directions: From intersection of US 93 and ID 75 near Challis, go southeast on US 93 and watch for signs to hot springs.

▲ Modern plumbing in the home does
▼ offer some rather strong pulsating showerheads, but they cannot even come close to the sensual liquid pounding which can be experienced in the hot waterfalls at *Goldbug Hot Springs*.

▲ *Challis Hot Springs:* This RV park with hookups and geothermal pools is a fine headquarters for vacationers.

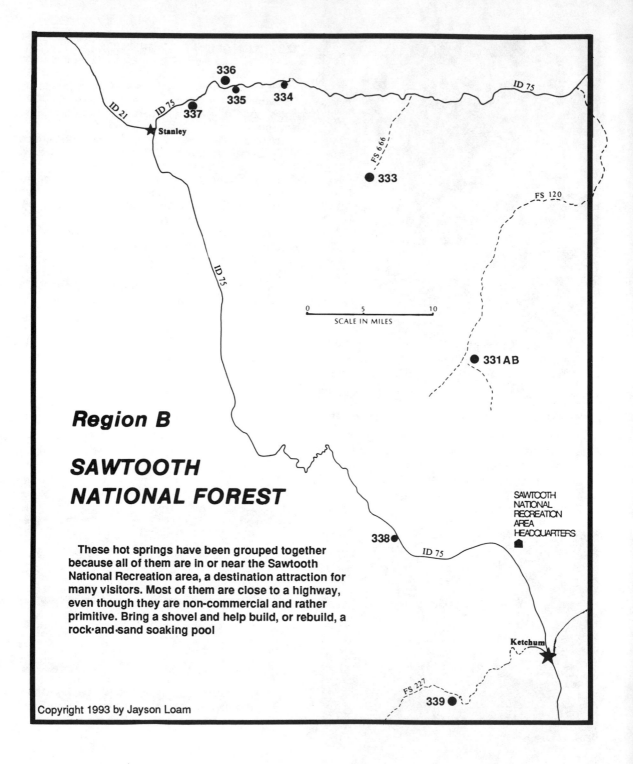

Region B

SAWTOOTH NATIONAL FOREST

These hot springs have been grouped together because all of them are in or near the Sawtooth National Recreation area, a destination attraction for many visitors. Most of them are close to a highway, even though they are non-commercial and rather primitive. Bring a shovel and help build, or rebuild, a rock-and-sand soaking pool

West Pass Hot Spring: A shot of the hills of Idaho as seen by a photographer floating in a bathtub-with-a-view.

331A WEST PASS HOT SPRING

● **Southeast of the town of Stanley**

A pair of out-in-the-open bathtubs along West Pass Creek, near an abandoned mine, in Sawtooth National Recreation Area. Elevation 7,000 ft. Road closed December 1 to May 1.

Natural mineral water flows out of a grassy hillside at 105º and runs continuously through a hose to the ancient bathtubs, which maintain a temperature of 102º. The apparent local custom in clothing optional.

There are no services on the premises. There is a walk-in campground within two miles and a drive-in campground within 30 miles. It is 34 miles to all other services in Clayton.

Directions: From ID 75, four miles east of Clayton, drive south on FS 120 along the East Fork of the Salmon River 29 miles to West Pass Creek. Cross the creek, drive 0.3 mile up hill and park on the flat area. Hike down a trail 20 yards past the abandoned mine to the springs.

Source map: *Sawtooth National Recreation Area.*

There are no traffic noises at *West Pass Hot Spring* to disturb a relaxed soaker.

▲ *Bowery Hot Spring:* This unique location offers both civilized soaking in a tub and primitive soaking in a rock pool.

331B   BOWERY HOT SPRING

● **Southeast of the town of Stanley**

An outdoor bathtub and a rock-and-sand soaking pool on the edge of the South Fork of the Salmon River in the Sawtooth National Recreation Area. Elevation 7,000 feet. Road closed December 1 to May 1.

Natural mineral water flows out of a spring at 125º and through a hose to the tub and the pool. Water temperature in the tub is controlled by diverting the hot water inflow. Water temperature in the volunteer-built primitive pool is controlled by admitting cold river water. The apparent local custom is clothing optional.

There are no services on the premises. There is a walk-in campground within two miles, and a drive-in campground within 30 miles. It is 34 miles to all other services in Clayton.

Directions: From ID 75, four miles east of Clayton, drive south on FS 120 along the East Fork of the Salmon River 30 miles to the parking lot at a trailhead. Hike 100 yards up the service road toward Bowery Forest Service Station. At the bridge, follow a trail upstream 100 yards to the spring.

333   SLATE CREEK HOT SPRING

● **Southeast of the town of Stanley**

A wooden soaking box and two rock-and-sand pools in a wooded canyon in the Sawtooth National Recreation Area. Elevation 7,000 ft. Open all year.

Natural mineral water flows out of a spring at 122º, and through a hose to the box, which is all that remains of a bathhouse that once stood near the HooDoo mine. Another hose brings cold water, permitting complete control of the water temperature in the box. There are also two primitive pools on the edge of the creek. The apparent local custom is clothing optional.

There are no services available on the premises. It is 17 miles to gas and a convenience store and 30 miles to all other services.

Directions: Drive 23 miles east of Stanley on ID 75. Turn right on FS 666 (Slate Creek Road) and drive 7.4 miles along Slate Creek to a closed gate at the HooDoo mine entrance. Park and walk up the road the remaining 500 yards to the spring.

Source map: *Sawtooth National Recreation Area.*

▲ *Sunbeam Hot Springs:* The parking lot and paved access path are visible on the other side of the morning steam plumes.

334 SUNBEAM HOT SPRINGS

● **East of the town of Stanley**

Several rock-and-sand pools on the edge of the Salmon River in Challis National Forest. Elevation 6,000 ft. Open all year.

Natural mineral water flows out of several springs on the north side of the road at temperatures up to 160º. The water flows under the road to several volunteer-built rock pools along the north bank of the river, where hot and cold water mix in a variety of temperatures. As all pools are easily visible from the road, bathing suits are advisable.

There are no services available on the premises. It is one mile to a store and cabins at Sunbeam Resort (summer only) and 11 miles to all other services in Stanley..

Location: On ID 75, one mile west of Sunbeam Resort, northeast of the town of Stanley.

Source map: *Sawtooth National Recreation Area.*

▲
▼ *Slate Creek Hot Spring:* The mine owners tried to keep soakers out of the old bathhouse, but decided that it was simpler to tear it down and ignore them.

▲ *Basin Creek Campground Hot Spring:* This location has a hot pool and a cool pool.

▲ *Kem (Basic Creek Bridge) Hot Springs:* This family-friendly location offers fishing, a campground, and a soaking pool.

335 KEM (BASIN CREEK BRIDGE) HOT SPRINGS

● **East of the town of Stanley**

Small, primitive spring and soaking pools on the edge of the Salmon River in Sawtooth National Recreation Area. Elevation 6,000 ft. Open all year.

Natural mineral water flows out of a spring at 110º and cools as it flows through several volunteer-built, rock-and-sand soaking pools along the edge of the river. Pool temperatures may be controlled by diverting the hot water or by bringing a bucket for adding cold river water. Because the spring is at the east end of a popular, unofficial campground, bathing suits are advisable in the daytime unless you check the situation out with your neighbors.

Except for the camping area, there are no services on the premises. It is seven miles to all services.

Directions: On ID 75, 0.7 of a mile east of mile marker 197, turn off the highway toward the river and down a short gravel road into the camping area.

Source map: *Sawtooth National Recreation Area* (hot springs not shown).

336 BASIN CREEK CAMPGROUND HOT SPRING

● **East of the town of Stanley**

Several shallow pools located on the edge of a creek adjacent to a campground in the Sawtooth National Recreation Area. Elevation 6,100 ft. Open all year.

Natural mineral water at 137º flows out of the ground and is mixed with cold creek water before flowing into several volunteer rock-and-sand pools. It is advisable to wear a bathing suit as the pools are near the campground.

There is an adjoining campground, and it is seven miles to all other services in Stanley.

Directions: Drive seven miles east of Stanley to Basin Creek Campground. Walk from campsite #4 through the bushes to the creek. The pools are hidden on the opposite side.

Source map: *Sawtooth National Forest* (hot springs not shown).

▲
►
Elkhorn Hot Spring: Adjusting the soaking temperature in the box requires just the right proportion of cold river water and scalding mineral water from the hose.

337 ELKHORN (BOAT BOX) HOT SPRING

● **East of the town of Stanley**

Small, wood soaking box perched on a rock between the road and the Salmon River in the Sawtooth National Recreation Area. Elevation 6,100 ft. Open all year.

Natural mineral water flows out of a spring at 136º and is piped under the road to the soaking box. The temperature in the box is varied by diverting the flow of hot water and pouring in buckets of cold river water. Bathing suits are advisable as the location is visible from the road.

There are no services on the premises. It is two miles to all services.

Directions: On ID 75, 0.7 of a mile east of mile marker 192, watch for a small turnout (two car limit) on the river side of the road. The box is visible from the turnout.

Source map: *Sawtooth National Recreation Area* (hot springs not shown).

338   RUSSIAN JOHN HOT SPRING

● **North of the town of Ketchum**

Remains of an old sheepherder soaking pool on a slope 200 yards above the highway in Sawtooth National Recreation Area. Elevation 6,900 ft. Open all year.

Natural mineral water flows out of a spring at 89º and directly into a small, clay-bottom pool which maintains a temperature of no more than 86º. Despite the cool temperature, this pool is so popular you may have to wait your turn. The apparent local custom is clothing optional.

There are no services available on the premises. It is 18 miles to all services.

Directions: On ID 75, 30 yards south of mile marker 146, turn west and then south to parking area.

Source map: *Sawtooth National Recreation Area.*

 Russian John Hot Spring: This easy-access idyllic spring has only one big drawback; you can't get warm in 86º water.

▲
►
Frenchman's Bend Hot Springs: The Forest Service has had to place restrictions on this delightful location to protect it from thoughtless party animals.

339   FRENCHMAN'S BEND HOT SPRING

● **West of the town of Ketchum.**

Several primitive roadside pools along both banks of Warm Springs Creek. Elevation 6,400 feet. Open all year for day use only.

Natural mineral water flows from the ground at more than 120º and into volunteer-built rock-and-sand pools where it is mixed with cold creek water to produce a comfortable soaking temperature. Nudity, alcohol, glass containers, non-biodegradable soap or shampoo and littering are prohibited.

There are no services on the premises. Roadside parking limitations must be observed. It is 11 miles to all services.

Directions: From ID 75 (Main Street) in Ketchum, drive 10.7 miles west on Warm Springs Road. Park in the well-marked parking area and walk 200 yards upstream to the spring.

Source Map: *Sawtooth National Recreation Area.*

◄ These pools at *Frenchman's Bend Hot Springs* are so popular that a parking area had to be built and signs posted.

Worswick Hot Springs: On a chilly day the entire upper slope is dotted with steam plumes from small geothermal fissures.

341   WORSWICK HOT SPRINGS

● **West of the town of Ketchum**

Dozens of primitive springs send a large flow of geothermal water tumbling down several acres of rolling hillside in the Sawtooth National Forest. Elevation 6,400 ft. Open all year.

Natural mineral water flows out of many springs at temperatures of more than 150º supplying a series of volunteer-built, rock-and-log pools in the drainage channels. The water cools as it flows downhill so the lower the pool the lower the temperature. The apparent local custom is clothing optional.

There are no services available on the premises. It is two miles to overnight camping and 14 miles to all other services.

Directions: From the intersection of FS 227 and FS 094, go 2.2 miles east of FS 227. Alternate route: From the town of Fairfield on US 20, go north on FS 094 to intersection with FS 227, the follow above directions.

Source map: *Sawtooth National Forest.*

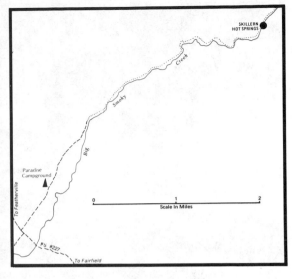

▲ *Preis Hot Spring:* Some volunteers get inspired to make a usable soaking pool from even a very small spring.

342   PREIS HOT SPRING

● **West of the town of Ketchum**

Small, two-person soaking box near the side of the road in Sawtooth National Forest. Elevation 6,000 ft. Open all year.

Natural mineral water flows out of the spring at 94º and directly into a small pool that has been given board sides and is large enough to accommodate two very friendly soakers. Bathing suits are advisable.

There are no services on the premises. It is two miles to overnight camping and 14 miles to all other services.

Directions: From the intersection of FS 227 and FS 094, go 2.1 miles north on FS 227 and watch for spring ten yards from the east side of the road. Alternate route: From the town of Fairfield on US 20, go north on FS 094 to intersection with FS 227, then follow above directions.

Source map: *Sawtooth National Forest.*

343   SKILLERN HOT SPRINGS

● **East of the town of Featherville**

Primitive hot spring on Big Smokey Creek, three miles by trail from Canyon Campground. Elevation 5,800 ft. Open all year.

Natural mineral water flows south from a spring at more than 110º, supplying a volunteer-built rock pool at the edge of the creek. Pool temperature is controllable by varying the amount of cold creek water admitted. The local custom is clothing optional.

There are no services on the premises. It is three miles to the campground and trailhead and 24 miles to all other services.

Directions: From Featherville, go 21 miles east on FS 227. About two miles beyond the South Fork Boise River, turn north to Canyon Campground. Trailhead is at the north end of the campground. The trail fords the stream several times and might not be passable during high water.

Source maps: *Sawtooth National Forest*; USGS *Sydney Butte* and *Paradise Peak, Idaho.*

344   BAUMGARTNER HOT SPRINGS

● **East of the town of Featherville**

Well-maintained soaking pool in popular Baumgartner Campground in Sawtooth National Forest. Elevation 5,000 ft. Open all year.

Natural mineral water flows out of a spring at 105º, supplying the soaking pool on a flow-through (no chlorine) basis and maintaining the temperature at 104º. Because of the pool's location in a campground, bathing suits are advisable.

Campground facilities are on the premises. It is 11 miles to a motel, restaurant, service station and grocery store, and 48 miles to RV hookups.

Location: On FS 227, 11 miles east of Featherville.

Source map: *Sawtooth National Forest.*

▲ *Baumgartner Hot Springs:* This pool is drained and cleaned daily, enabling flow-through use without chlorination.

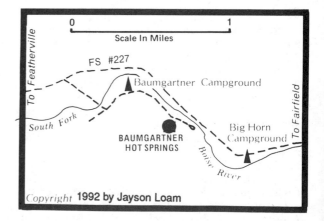

 Willow Creek Hot Springs: At the end of the valley hot water runs through this lovely pool before joining the creek.

345 WILLOW CREEK HOT SPRINGS

● **East of the town of Featherville**

A series of primitive soaking pools in a lovely small alpine valley in the Sawtooth National Forest. Elevation 5,200 feet. Open all year.

Natural mineral water flows out of the ground at 125º and runs 100 yards across a gravel bar to join the creek. Volunteers have built a large rock-and-sand soaking pool where the water has cooled to 105º and a smaller one where the water has cooled to 96º. The apparent local custom is clothing optional.

There are no services available at the spring, but there is a campground at the trailhead. It is 10 miles to other services in Featherville, and 47 miles to RV hookups.

Directions: From Featherville, drive seven miles east on FS 227 to Willow Creek, then two miles north on FS 008 to the campground and trailhead. The spring is .75 mile north on a moderate, well-maintained trail.

Source map: *Sawtooth National Forest.*

In the upper part, where the the runoff from *Willow Creek Hot Springs* has cooled to 105º, volunteers have used logs to build this rustic soaking pool.

▲ *Green Canyon Hot Springs:* The original indoor swimming pool, with its snack bar and arcade is a year-round social center.

▼ The newer hydrojet pool at *Green Canyon Hot Springs* is designed to accommodate dozens of families on busy weekends.

351   GREEN CANYON HOT SPRINGS
■ Box 96   (208) 458-4454
   Newdale, ID 83436   PR+CRV

Rural, indoor plunge and RV park in a really green canyon. Elevation 6,000 ft. Open every day except Sunday from mid-April to the end of September; open weekends the rest of the year.

Natural mineral water flows out of a spring at 118º and is piped to pools and a geothermal greenhouse. The indoor swimming pool is maintained at 90º, and the outdoor hydrojet pool is maintained at 105º. Both pools are treated with chlorine, and bathing suits are required.

Locker rooms, snack bar, picnic area and RV hookups are available on the premises. It is 21 miles to all other services. No credit cards are accepted.

Directions: From the town of Driggs, go north and west 17 miles on ID 33. At Canyon Creek bridge, turn south and follow signs four miles to resort.

▲
►
This covered hot pool at *Heise Hot Springs* stays open all year but the big swimming pool is for summer use only.

---

352 HEISE HOT SPRINGS
■ Box 417   (208) 538-7312
   Ririe, ID   PR+CRV

Modernized, family-oriented resort with spacious, tree-shaded picnic and RV grounds on the north bank of the Snake River. Elevation 5,000 ft. Open all year except the month of November.

Natural mineral water flows out of a spring at 126º and is piped to an enclosed hydrojet pool which is maintained at 105ºand requires no chemical treatment required. Tap water, treated with chlorine and heated by geothermal heat exchangers, is used in the other pools. An outdoor soaking pool is maintained at 92-93º, the large swimming pool at 82º, and the waterslide pick-up pool at 85º. Bathing suits are required in all areas.

Locker rooms, cafe, overnight camping, RV hookups, picnic area and golf course are available on the premises. It is five miles to a store, service station and motel. No credit cards are accepted.

Directions: From the town of Idaho Falls, go east 22 miles on US 26 and then follow signs four miles north across river to resort.

Lava Hot Springs Foundation: This is one of the smaller pools which is cooled by a refreshing cold water shower.

◄ The Olympic-size swimming pool is equipped for diving competition.

353A LAVA HOT SPRINGS FOUNDATION
P.O. Box 669 **(800) 423-8597**
■ Lava Hot Springs, ID 83246 **PR**

Two attractive and well-maintained recreation areas operated by a self-supporting state agency in the town of Lava Hot Springs. Elevation 5,000 ft.

GEOTHERMAL POOLS: (East end of town; open 363 days per year.) Natural mineral water flows out of the ground at 112º and directly up through the gravel bottoms of a Roman-style pool in a sunken garden and a large, partly shaded soaking pool. No chemical treatment is necessary. Pool temperatures range down to 107º at the drain end of the soaking pool. The same water is pumped to two partly shaded hydrojet pools where cold shower water may be added to control the pool temperature. Bathing suits are required. Massage is available on the premises.

SWIMMING POOLS: (West end of town; open Memorial Day to Labor Day.) Hot mineral water is piped from the geothermal springs and flows continuously through the TAC-size pool and the Olypmic-size pool, maintaining a temperature of 80º. The pool complex is surrounded by a large, level lawn. Bathing suits are required.

Locker rooms are available at both locations, and it is less than three blocks to all other services. No credit cards are accepted.

▲ The main pools at *Lava Hot Springs Foundation* are surrounded by green lawns, sun decks and landscaping.

▼ *Riverside Inn:* This hot tub was added to accomodate those guests who wanted to soak out in the fresh air and sunshine.

353B RIVERSIDE INN

255 Portneuf Ave.   **(800) 773-5504**
Lava Hot Springs, ID 83246   **PR+MH**

A faithfully restored historic hotel, once known as the *Elegant Grand Inn*, visible on the main street between the two Lava Hot Springs Foundation locations. Elevation 5,400 ft. Open all year.

Natural mineral water Is pumped out of a well at 133º, diluted with cold water down to 104º, then piped to three indoor private soaking pools and an outdoor soaking pool overlooking the Portneuf River. Because the pools operate on a continuous flow-through basis, no chemical treatment of the water is needed. The pools are available to the public as well as to registered guests.

Modernized hotel rooms are available on the non-smoking premises. It is less than three blocks to all other services. Visa MasterCard and Discover are accepted.

353C HOME HOTEL AND MOTEL

306 E. Main   **(208) 776-5507**
Lava Hot Springs, ID 83246   **MH**

Remodeled, older hotel featuring hot mineral baths in all units, on the main street between the two Lava Hot Springs Foundation locations. Elevation 5,400 ft. Open all year.

Natural mineral water flows out of a spring at 121º and is piped to two-person tubs in all rooms, and in a rental house. Temperature in each tub is controllable by the customer. The eight rooms in the hotel are non-smoking; the 13 rooms in the motel section permit smoking.

It is less than three blocks to a cafe, store, service station, overnight camping and RV hookups. Visa and MasterCard are accepted.

355 RIVERDALE RESORT
3696 N. 1600 E.   (208) 852-0266
Preston, ID 83263   PR+CRV

New commercial development in a rural valley subdivision. Elevation 4,000 ft. Open all year.

Natural mineral water is pumped from a geothermal well at 112º, then piped to various outdoor pools. All soaking pools are flow-through and drained daily, eliminating the need for chemical treatment of the water. The partly shaded hydrojet pool is maintained at 103-105º, and a large soaking pool is maintained at 97-100º in the summer and 102-104º in the winter. The chlorinated junior Olympic swimming pool is maintained at 86º in the summer. A chlorinated waterslide catch pool is maintained at approximately 80º. Bathing suits are required.

Locker rooms, snack bar, overnight camping and RV hookups are available on the premises. It is less than six miles to a cafe, store, service station and motel. Visa and MasterCard are accepted.

Directions: From Preston on US 91, go 6 miles north on ID 34 and watch for resort signs.

Riverdale Resort: For the young and active customers, there is an exciting water slide and a large swimming pool with lifeguard. There are also several separate smaller soaking pools where parents can take their small fry for inner tube and splashing lessons.

354 BEAR LAKE HOT SPRINGS
Box 75   (208) 945-2494
St. Charles, ID 83272   PR+CRV

Large pool building and campground on a remote section of the lakeshore. Elevation 6,000 ft. Open May to September.

Natural mineral water flows out of a spring at 120º and is piped to two indoor pools which operate on a flow-through basis requiring no chemical treatment. The swimming pool is maintained at 75-85º and the ten-person soaking pool at 110-115º. Bathing suits are required.

Locker rooms, cafe, overnight parking and a boat dock are on the premises. It is seven miles to a store, service station and motel. No credit cards are accepted.

Directions: From US 89 on the north side of the town of St. Charles, follow signs across the north end of Bear Lake to the resort.

Downnata Hot Springs: When this superslide is in use there is always an attendant on duty at the catch pool.

The main swimming pool at *Downata Hot Springs* offers a choice of smaller slides and a tilting float in the center.

356 DOWNATA HOT SPRINGS

25901 Downata Rd. (208) 897-5736
Downey, ID 83234 PR+CRV

Expanded, older, rural plunge and picnic grounds in the rolling hills of southeastern Idaho. Elevation 4,000 ft. Open Memorial Day to Labor Day.

Natural mineral water flows out of a spring at 112° and is piped to outdoor pools treated with chlorine. The main swimming pool and the waterslide catch pool are maintained at 85-95º. Bathing suits are required.

Locker rooms, snack bar, picnic grounds, overnight camping sand volleyball court are available on the premises. It is three miles to a store, service stations and motel. No credit cards are accepted.

Directions: On US 91, drive 3 miles south from the town of Downey and watch for signs.

▲
► *Indian Springs Natatorium*: Convenient changing rooms are built into the fence surrounding this community plunge.

357   INDIAN SPRINGS NATATORIUM
■   3249 Indian Springs Rd.   (208) 226-2174
        American Falls, ID 83211   PR+CRV

Older, rural picnic ground and plunge with RV accommodations. Elevation 5,200 ft. Open April 1 to Labor Day.

Natural mineral water flows out of a spring at 90º and is piped to an outdoor swimming pool which is treated with chlorine and maintains a temperature of 90º. Bathing suits are required.

Locker rooms, picnic area and full-hookup RV spaces are available on the premises. It is three miles to all other services. No credit cards are accepted.

Location: On Idaho Route 37, three miles south of the city of American Falls.

▲
► *Nat-Soo-Pah Hot Springs:* The smaller specialized pools and water slide supplement the large swimming pool.

358   NAT-SOO-PAH HOT SPRINGS
■ 2738 E 2400 N   (208) 655-4337
   Hollister, ID 83301   PR+CRV

Clean and quiet community plunge with soaking pools and acres of tree-shaded grass for picnics and overnight camping. Located on the Snake River plain, south of Twin Falls. Elevation 4,400 ft. Open May 1 to Labor Day.

Natural mineral water flows out of a spring at 99º and is piped to three outdoor pools. The swimming pool is maintained at 92-94º, using flow-through and some chlorine treatment. Part of the swimming pool flow-through is heated with a heat pump to supply the soaking pool which is maintained at a temperature of 104-106º. The hydrojet pool, supplied by direct flow-through from the spring, maintains a temperature of 99º and requires no chemical treatment. There is also a small waterslide at the side of the swimming pool. Bathing suits are required.

Locker rooms, snack bar, picnic area, overnight camping and RV hookups are available on the premises. It is four miles to a store and service station and 16 miles to a motel. No credit cards are accepted.

Directions: From US 93, 1/2 mile south of Hollister and 1/2 mile north of the Port of Entry, go east three miles on Nat-Soo-Pah Road directly into the location.

▲ The roman-type indoor pools at *Banbury Hot Springs* are large enough a family.

▲ *Banbury Hot Springs:* This fine vacation spot offers a boat dock and shaded RV spaces in addition to many hot pools.

359A   BANBURY HOT SPRINGS
Route 3   **(208) 543-4098**
■ **Buhl, ID 83316**   **PR+CRV**

Community plunge on the Snake River with soaking pools and spacious, tree-shaded area for picnics and overnight camping. Elevation 3,000 ft. Open mid-May to Labor Day.

Natural mineral water flows out of a spring at 141º and is piped to a large, outdoor, chlorine-treated pool which is maintained at a temperature of 89º-95º. Mineral water is also piped to ten private-space soaking pools, some equipped with hydrojets. Water temperature in each pool is individually controlled. Each soaking pool is drained, cleaned and refilled after each use, so no chemical treatment of the water is needed. Bathing suits are required except in private space pools.

Locker rooms, snack bar, overnight camping, RV hookups, and a boat ramp and dock are located on the premises. It is four miles to a restaurant and 12 miles to a store, service station and motel. No credit cards are accepted.

Directions: From the town of Buhl, go ten miles north on US 30. Watch for sign and turn east 1 1/2 miles to resort.

120

Miracle Hot Springs: Every morning a group of local seniors gets their morning exercise in the main swimming pool.

In the private space pools at *Miracle Hot Springs,* the amount of flow-through hot water may be adjusted by the customer.

359B   MIRACLE HOT SPRINGS

Route 3 Box 171   **(208) 543-6002**
Buhl, ID 83316   **PR+CRV**

Older health spa surrounded by rolling agricultural land. Elevation 3,000 ft. Open all year.

Natural mineral water is pumped out of a well at 139º and into an outdoor swimming pool and 19 roofless, enclosed soaking pools, all of which operate on a flow-through basis requiring no chemical treatment. The swimming pool is maintained at a temperature of 95º, and the temperature in the individual pools is controllable. Bathing suits are required in public areas. All buildings and dressing rooms are supplied with geothermal heat.

Massage by appointment, RV hookups and overnight camping are available on the premises. A restaurant is available within three miles, and all other services are available within ten miles. No credit cards are accepted.

Location: On US 30, ten miles north of the town of Buhl.

Some of the indoor pools at *Sligar's Thouand Springs Resort* are large enough to hold more than a dozen soakers.

▲ *Sligar's Thousand Springs Resort:* It is a challenge to play water polo keep-away while balancing on the tethered log.

---

360   SLIGAR'S THOUSAND SPRINGS RESORT

■ **Route 1, Box 90**   (208) 837-4987
Hagerman, ID 83332   **PR+CRV**

Indoor plunge with private-space hydrojet tubs and green, shaded RV park with a view of multiple waterfalls on cliffs across the Snake River. Elevation 2,900 ft. Open all year.

Natural mineral water flows out of a spring at 200º and is piped to an indoor swimming pool, 17 indoor hydrojet pools large enough for eight people, and one indoor hydrojet pool large enough for 20 people. The temperature in the swimming pool is maintained between 90-96º, while the temperature in the hydrojet pools is individually controllable. All the pools are chlorinated. Bathing suits are required in public areas.

Locker rooms, boat dock, shaded picnic area, overnight camping and RV hookups are available on the premises. A restaurant is within one mile, and all other services are within 5 miles. No credit cards are accepted.

Directions: On US 30, eight miles south of the town of Hagerman.

▶ *Murphy's Hot Springs:* The meandering river alongside the pool is just right for this remote informal outpost.

361   MURPHY'S HOT SPRINGS

■   **Rogerson, ID 83302**   **(208) 857-2233**
                                  PR+MH+CRV

Western-style pool, bathhouse, bar and RV park in a remote section of the Jarbridge River Canyon. Elevation 5,100 ft. Open all year.

Natural mineral water flows out of two springs at 129º and into an outdoor, chlorine-treated pool and into three indoor, flow-through soaking pools requiring no chemicals. The swimming pool is maintained at temperatures ranging from 80-90º. The large indoor pool for use by six people is maintained at 96º, and the two smaller, two-person tubs are maintained at 104º and 107º. Pools are open to the public in addition to registered guests. Bathing suits are required in the pool and public areas.

Dressing rooms, cafe, gas pump, cabins, overnight camping and RV hookups are available on the premises. It is 49 miles to a store and service station. No credit cards are accepted.

Directions: From Twin Falls, go approximately 37 miles south on US 93. Watch for highway sign and turn southwest 1/2 mile into Rogerson. At main intersection, watch for Murphy Hot Springs highway sign and follow signs 49 miles to location. Only the last few miles are gravel.

NO RUNNING

▲ *Givens Hot Springs:* The activity program
at this community recreation and social
◀ center includes group and individual
swimming instruction for all ages.

362　GIVENS HOT SPRINGS

■

HC 79 Box 103	(208) 495-2000
Melba, ID 83641	PR+CRV

Rural plunge, picnic grounds and RV park on
agricultural plateau above the Snake River.
Elevation 3,000 ft. Open all year.

Natural mineral water flows out of an artesian
spring at 120º and is piped to a chlorine-treated,
indoor swimming pool and six indoor, private-space
soaking pools which operate on a drain-and-fill
basis requiring no chemicals. The swimming pool is
maintained at a temperature of 99º in the winter
and 85º in the summer. The temperature in the tubs
is individually controllable, with temperatures
ranging from 105-110º. Bathing suits are required.

Dressing rooms, a snack bar, picnic grounds,
softball diamond and overnight camping are
available on the premises. It is 11 miles to all other
services. Visa and MasterCard are accepted.

Location: Eleven miles southeast of the town of
Marsing on ID 78.

▲
◀ *Warm Springs Resort:* This location has one of the largest flow-through (no chlorination) swimming pools in Idaho.

363 WARM SPRINGS RESORT
■ P.O. Box 28   (208) 392-4437
Idaho City, ID 86361   PR+MH+CRV

Rural plunge and RV park surrounded by Boise National Forest. Elevation 4,000 ft. Open all year.

Natural mineral water flows out of a spring at 110º and through an outdoor swimming pool maintained at a temperature of 94º in summer and 97º in winter. Chemical treatment of the water is not required. The pool is open to the public as well as to registered guests. Bathing suits are required.

Locker rooms, snack bar, cabins, overnight camping and RV hookups are available on the premises. A cafe, store and service station are located within two miles. No credit cards are accepted.

Location: On ID 21, 1 1/2 miles south of Idaho City.

Region C BOISE RIVER — MIDDLE FORK

The common thread connecting these hot springs is a gravel road FS 268, which winds along the riverbank for 50 miles, often only one lane wide. Loaded logging trucks coming downstream have the inside lane, while upstream traffic must make do with turnouts on the edge toward the river— not recommended for trailers and motor homes. It is possible to reach Atlanta by taking FS 384, FS 327 and FS 268 from ID 21, 15 miles south of Lowman. Then, when you head downstream from Atlanta to Arrowroot Reservoir on FS 268, you will at least have the inside lane and will not be meeting any loaded logging trucks.

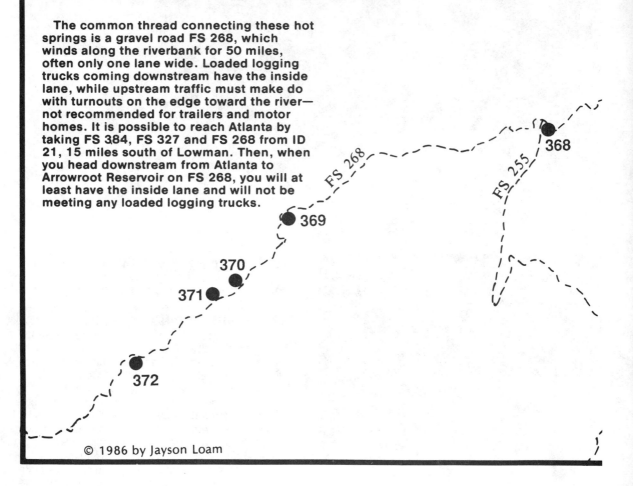

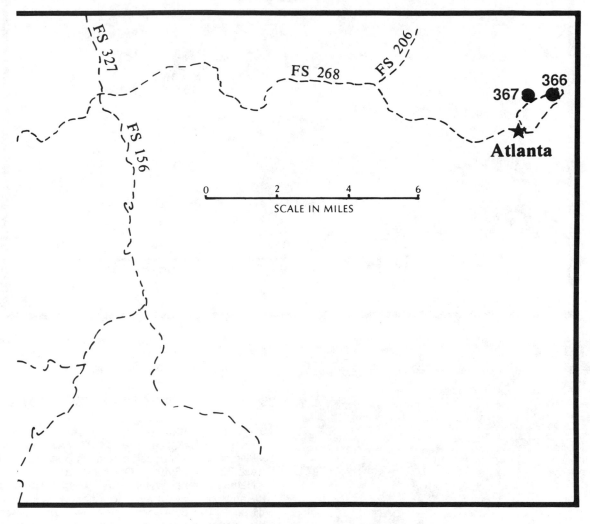

The hot springs below are listed in sequence, working downstream from Atlanta Hot Springs.

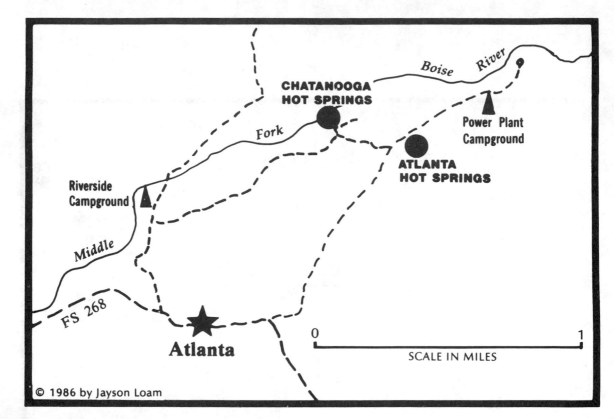

© 1986 by Jayson Loam

◄ *Atlanta Hot Springs:* Runoff from this hot mineral water pool flows to the larger cold pond visible across the road.

---

366   ATLANTA HOT SPRINGS (see map)

● **North of the town of Atlanta**

Primitive spring and a small, rock-and-sand soaking pool on a wooded plateau in Boise National Forest. Elevation 5,400 ft. Open all year.

Natural mineral water flows out of a spring at 110º and cools as it travels to a nearby, volunteer-built pool. The pool temperature is approximately 100º, depending on air temperature and wind conditions. This site is easily visible from the nearby road, so bathing suits are advisable.

No services are on the premises.

It is one-half mile to a campground, one mile to cabins, cafe, service station and store, and 62 miles to RV hookups.

Source maps: *Boise National Forest;* USGS *Atlanta East* and *Atlanta West.*

367 CHATANOOGA HOT SPRINGS
(see map)

● **North of the town of Atlanta**

Large, comfortable, sand-bottom pool at the foot of a geothermal cliff surrounded by the tree-covered slopes of Boise National Forest. Elevation 5,400 ft. Open all year.

Natural mineral water flows out of fissures in a 100-foot high cliff at 120º and cools as it tumbles toward a volunteer-built, rock-and-sand soaking pool which retains a temperature of more than 100º. The apparent local custom is clothing optional.

There are no services on the premises. It is one-half mile to a campground, one mile to a cafe, cabins, service station and store, and 62 miles to RV hookups.

Note: The pool is visible from the north edge of the unmarked parking area at the top of the cliff. Several well-worn, steep paths lead down to the pool.

Source maps: *Boise National Forest;* USGS *Atlanta East* and *Atlanta West.*

Chatanooga Hot Springs: This site, with its natural cooling-tower cascade, has one of the most dramatic Idaho settings.

Dutch Frank Hot Springs: This bubbling riverbank has unlimited possibilities.

Loftus Hot Springs: Volunteers have prepared this charming grotto with waterfall for peaceful meditation.

Smith Cabin Hot Springs: A little more work is needed on this shallow pool.

368 DUTCH FRANK HOT SPRINGS
(see map)

Scattered, geothermal flows along 200 yards of riverbank. Located on the south bank of the river, immediately east of the Roaring River bridge.

369 NEINMEYER HOT SPRINGS
(see map)

Several primitive hot springs on the south bank of the river, across from Neinmeyer Campground.

370 LOFTUS HOT SPRINGS (see map)

Intimate, leafy, volunteer-built soaking pool with 100º water, ten yards from a small parking area on the north side of the road. It is located 0.2 of a mile east of the bridge (see map).

371 SMITH CABIN HOT SPRINGS
(see map)

Volunteer-built, river's-edge pools on both sides of the river, 0.7 of a mile west of the above described bridge.

372 SHEEP CREEK BRIDGE HOT SPRINGS (see map)

Volunteer-built pool with rock screen containing algae-laden water at temperatures up to 100º, depending on weather conditions. It is located 20 yards from the south end of the bridge over which the road returns to the north side of the river.

 Sheep Creek Bridge Hot Springs: One of the plentiful, but seldom used, non-commercial hot springs along this river.

356 SAWTOOTH LODGE

(208) 259-3331
Grandjean, ID 83637   **PR+MH+CRV**

Historic, mountain resort in the Sawtooth Recreation Area. Elevation 5,100. Open June through October.

Natural mineral water flows out of several springs with temperatures up to 150º and into an outdoor, chlorinated swimming pool maintained at approximately 80º. The pool is available to the public as well as to registered guests. Bathing suits are required.

Dressing rooms, cafe, cabins, overnight camping and RV hookups are available on the premises. It is 28 miles to a store and service station. Visa and MasterCard are accepted.

Directions: From the town of Lowman, go 22 miles east on ID 21, then follow signs six miles on gravel road to lodge.

Sawtooth Lodge: This modern pool is for those who are unable to be comfortable in a squishy-bottom hot spring.

357 SACAJAWEA HOT SPRINGS

West of the town of Grandjean

Popular, large geothermal area on the north bank of the South Fork of the Payette River in Boise National Forest. Elevation 5,000 ft. Open all year.

Natural mineral water flows out of many springs at temperatures up to 108º and cools as it cascades into a series of volunteer-built rock pools along the river's edge. Because the pools are visible from the road, bathing suits are advisable.

There are no services available on the premises. It is one mile to a cafe, cabins, overnight camping and RV hookups, and 27 miles to a store and service station.

Directions: From Lowman, drive 21 miles east on ID 21 to Grandjean turnoff (FS 524) on rights. Follow gravel road 4.6 miles to Wapiti Creek Bridge. Look for springs on right side of read, 0.6 of a mile past the bridge.

▲ Runoff from *Sacajawea Hot Springs* fills the
warm water pool enjoyed by the family
while father fishes in the cold stream.

Bonneville Hot Springs: Volunteers have built this large sandy-bottom pool where the scalding geothermal water can be combined with cold creek water to maintain a temperature around 95º.

● **West of the town of Grandjean**

Popular, semi-remote geothermal area on a tree-lined creek in Boise National Forest. Elevation 4,800 ft. Open all year.

Natural mineral water flows out of a multitude of springs with various temperatures up to 180º. Be careful not to step into any of the scalding runoff channels. There is one small, wooden bathhouse with an individual tub supplied from a nearby spring at a temperature of 103º. Soakers drain the tub after each use. There are also many volunteer-built, rock-and-sand soaking pools along the edge of the creek where the geothermal water can be mixed with cold water. Bathing suits are advisable.

No services are available on the premises. It is one-quarter mile to a campground, eight miles to cafe, cabins and RV hookups, and 19 miles to a store and service station.

Directions: From Lowman, drive 19 miles northeast to Bonneville Campground (formerly Warm Springs Campground). From the north edge of the campground, follow the unmarked but well-worn path 1/4 mile to geothermal area.

Several other smaller soaking pools have been built where *Bonneville Hot Springs* geothermal water can be mixed with cold fresh water.

Kirkham Hot Springs: Insects destroyed many of the trees, but this location still has a campground and hot mineral water showers available 24 hours per day.

380   KIRKHAM HOT SPRINGS

● **East of the town of Lowman**

Popular geothermal area with many hot waterfalls and pools adjoining a National Forest campground on the South Fork of the Payette River. Elevation 4,200 ft. Open all year.

Natural mineral water flows out of many springs and fissures along the south bank of the river a temperatures up to 120º and cools as it cascades toward the river. Volunteers have built several rock-and-sand soaking pools in which temperatures can vary above or below 100º depending on air temperature and wind conditions. Bathing suits are advisable, especially in the daytime.

Overnight camping is available in the adjoining campground. It is four mile to a cafe, store, service station and cabins, and 34 miles to RV hookups.

Directions: From the town of Lowman, go four miles east on ID 21 and watch for Kirkham Hot Springs Campground sign.

Source map: *Boise National Forest*.

381 PINE FLATS HOT SPRING

● **West of the town of Lowman**

Spectacular, geothermal cascade and cliffside soaking pool overlooking the South Fork of the Payette River in Boise National Forest. Elevation 4,100 ft. Open all year.

Natural mineral water with temperatures up to 125º flows from several springs on top of a one-hundred-foot high cliff, cooling as it spills and tumbles over the rocks. There is one volunteer-built, tarp-lined rock pool 30 feet above the river immediately below a hot shower-bath which averages 104º. Other rock pools at the foot of the cliff have lower temperatures. The apparent local custom is clothing optional.

The hot springs are located one-third mile from the Pine Flats Campground and parking area. It is four miles to a cafe, store, service station and motel, and 27 miles to RV hookups.

Directions: From the west edge of Pine Flats campground, follow an unmarked but well-worn path 1/3 mile west down to and along a large riverbed, rock-and-sand bar. Look for geothermal water cascading down the cliff onto the bar.

Source map: *Boise National Forest.*

▲
▶
Pine Flats Hot Spring: Volunteers have built this unique pool on a rocky cliff where geothermal water cascades in at 105º. A shallow warm play pool, just right for toddlers, is formed at the edge of the river by the hot water runoff.

Hot Springs Campground: Volunteers build their pools by the foundation of an old bathhouse which was destroyed long ago.

383   DEER CREEK HOT SPRINGS

● **West of the town of Crouch**

Small, volunteer-built soaking pool in a gully 20 yards from a paved highway, combining the flow from several springs, a test well and a creek. Elevation 3,000 ft. Open all year.

Natural mineral water flows out of multiple springs and an abandoned well casing at temperatures ranging up to 176º. Volunteers have built a shallow, plastic-and-sand soaking pool on one side of the creek to mix the hot and cold water. There are no posted clothing requirements, but the proximity to the highway makes bathing suits advisable.

There are no services available on the premises, but all services are available four miles away.

Directions: From the town of Crouch, go 4 1/2 miles west toward the town of Banks, watching for a steep dirt road on the north side of the highway. Do not drive up the road—it deadends in just a few yards. Park in a turnout on the river side of the highway and walk back to the springs, which are just below the steep side road.

Source map: *Boise National Forest.*

382   HOT SPRINGS CAMPGROUND

● **East of the town of Crouch**

The cement foundations of a long-gone bathhouse and some small, volunteer-built soaking pools are intended to use some of the continuing hot-water flow. Located on a riverbank across the highway from a National Forest campground. Elevation 3,800 ft. Open all year.

Natural mineral water flows out of several springs at 105º and into volunteer-built, shallow, rock-and-sand pools near the south side of the highway. Bathing suits are advisable.

Overnight camping is available on the premises. All other services are available four miles away.

Directions: From the town of Crouch, go four miles east toward Lowman. Look for Hot Springs Campground one mile after entering Forest Service land.

Source map: *Boise National Forest.*

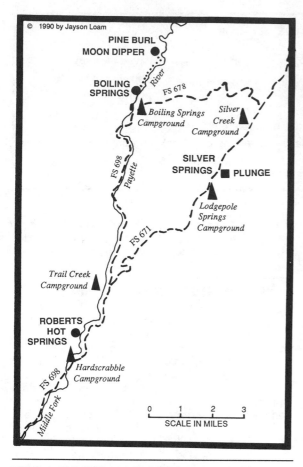

Rocky Canyon Hot Spring: Volunteers use some form of tarp to hold the water when they build a pool above river level.

384   ROCKY CANYON (ROBERTS) HOT SPRING

(see map)

North of the town of Crouch

Primitive hot spring on the Middle Fork of the Payette River in Boise National Forest. Elevation 4,000 ft. Open all year.

Natural mineral water flows out of a spring at 120º, then down a steep slope toward the river. To reach the spring, you must ford the river, which might not be safe during high water. Volunteers have built a series of primitive rock pools, each colder that the one above. All pools are visible from the road, so bathing suits are advisable.

There are no services available on the premises. It is 1/2 mile to a picnic area, one mile to a campground, and ten miles to all other services in Crouch.

Source map: *Boise National Forest.*

385   BOILING SPRINGS   (see map)

North of the town of Crouch

Large, geothermal water flow on the Middle Fork of the Payette River in Boise National Forest. Elevation 4,200 ft. Open all year.

Natural mineral water flows out of a cliff at more than 130º, into a pond adjacent to the Boiling Springs guard station. The water cools as it flows through a ditch to join the river. Summer volunteers usually build a rock-and-mud dam at he point where the water is cool enough for soaking. Because of the nearby campground, bathing suits are advisable.

No services are available on the premises. It is one-quarter mile to a campground and 19 miles to all other services.

Directions: From the north edge of Boiling Springs campground, follow the path 1/4 mile to the guard station and spring.

Source map: *Boise National Forest.*

Moon Dipper Hot Spring: Adding creek water controls this pool's temperature, but *Pine Burl's* temperatures is controlled by diverting the hot water.

386A MOON DIPPER HOT SPRING AND
386B PINE BURL HOT SPRING
(see map on preceding page)

● **North of the town of Crouch**

Two remote and primitve hot springs on the bank of Dash Creek, very close together in Boise National Forest. Elevation 4,200 ft. Open all year.

Natural mineral water flows out of two springs at 120º and directly into volunteer-built, rock soaking pools. Water temperature in the pools in controlled by mixing cold creek water with the hot water. The apparent local custom is clothing optional.

No services are available on the premises. It is a two-mile hike to overnight camping and 21 miles to all other services.

Directions: From the Boiling Springs guard station, follow a well-used but unmarked path along the river for a a two-mile hike to the springs.

Source maps: *Boise National Forest;* USGS *Boiling Springs, Idaho.*

Note: There are several more primitive hot springs with potential for volunteer-built soaking pools further upstream from Moon Dipper and Pine Burl. However, all of them require that the river be forded many times with a high risk of losing the faint, unmarked path. Consult with a Boise National Forest ranger before attempting to hike to any of these springs.

Silver Creek Plunge: This very large warm water pool, in which innertubes are permitted, is great for teenagers.

387 SILVER CREEK PLUNGE
(208) 344-8688 (unit 1942)
H/C 76 Box 237
Garden Valley, ID 83622   PR+MH+CRV

Remote, mountain resort surrounded by Boise National Forest. Elevation 4,600 ft. Open all year; snowmobile access in winter.

Natural mineral water flows out of a spring at 101º directly into an outdoor swimming pool which is maintained at 84º. The pool operates on a flow-through basis so it requires a minimum of chlorination. It is available to the public as well as to registered guests. Bathing suits are required.

Dressing rooms, snack bar, cabins and overnight camping are available on the premises. It is 22 miles to a store, service station and RV hookups. No credit cards are accepted.

Directions: From the town of Crouch, go north 14 miles on FS 698, then bear northeast on FS 671 for nine miles to plunge.

Source map: *Boise National Forest.*

388 BREIT (TRAIL CREEK) HOT SPRING
(see map)
West of Warm Lake

Small, beautiful hot spring and soaking pool in a narrow canyon down a steep, 60-yard path from a paved highway in Boise National Forest. Elevation 6,000 ft. Open all year.

Natural mineral water flows out of a fissure in the rocks adjoining Trail Creek at 125º. Volunteers have placed a white enamel bathtub in the creekbed and installed a hose to bring in this hot water. Bring a bucket with which to add cold creek water when desired. Volunteers have also built a primitive, rock-and-sand soaking pool on the edge of the creek where the temperature can be controlled by changing the amount of cold creek water admitted. The apparent local custom is clothing optional.

No services are available on the premises. It is two miles to a campground, 7 miles to gas, cafe, cabins and phone at Warm Lake Lodge (open Memorial Day to October 15.) and 22 miles to all other services in Cascade..

Directions: from the intersection of FS 22 and FS 474 west of Warm Lake, go west 3.7 miles and look for an especially large parking area on the south side of the road. From the west edge of this parking area, the pool is visible at the bottom of Trail Creek canyon. There is no maintained trail, so be careful scrambling down the steep path.

Source map: *Boise National Forest.*

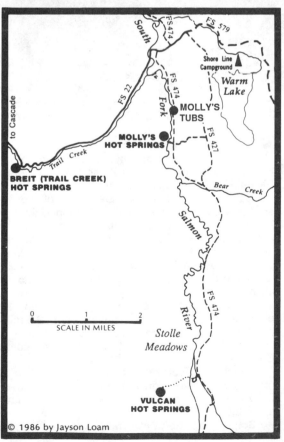

▲ *Breit Hot Spring:* A hot spring with a bathtub is called "Yuppie Primitive".

▼ The source spring is visible in this photo taken from the parking area.

© 1986 by Jayson Loam

141 IDAHO

Molly's Tubs: Volunteer "engineers" have spent years dragging in the tubs and spreading a Mickey Mouse maze of hot water collection pipes over the hillside.

---

389 A   MOLLY'S TUBS   (see map)

● **West of Warm Lake**

A much used collection of bathtubs on the South Fork of the Salmon River in Boise National Forest. Elevation 5,200 ft. Open all year.

Natural mineral water flows out of several springs at approximately 120º and is piped through hoses to eight bathtubs. Buckets are used for adding cold water from the nearby river. The tubs are lined up in two groups so you can have relative privacy if desired. Take a roll of duct tape for sealing leaks and drain holes. The apparent local custom is clothing optional.

There are no services available on the premises. It is 1.5 miles to a campground, 3.5 miles to Warm Lake Lodge (open Memorial Day to October 15) and 24 miles to all other services in Cascade.

Directions: From the intersection of FS 22 (paved) and FS 474 (gravel), go 1.3 miles south on FS 474 to pullout on right. Follow a steep path down to the tubs.

Source map: *Boise National Forest.*

389B   MOLLY'S HOT SPRING   (see map)

● **West of Warm Lake**

A tarp-lined pool on the side of a steep, geothermal hillside overlooking the South Fork of the Salmon River in Boise National Forest. Locals named this one "the Duke" in honor of repeated visits from John Wayne and Robert Mitchum. Elevation 5,400 ft. Open all year.

Natural mineral water flows out of several springs at temperatures up to 120º and is transported downhill by a variety of pipes and hoses. Water temperature in the volunteer-built pool is controlled by diverting or combining the hotter and cooler flows. Additional volunteer work could produce an excellent chest-deep pool. The apparent local custom is clothing optional.

No services are available on the premises. It is three miles to overnight camping, five miles to gas, cafe, store, cabins and phone at Warm Lake Lodge (open Memorial Day to October 15) and 25 miles to all other services in Cascade.

Directions: From the intersection of FS 22 (paved) and FS 474 (gravel), go 1.7 miles south on FS 474 to intersection with a road signed east to Warm Lake. The road leading west from this intersection has been blocked to vehicle traffic, but it is passable on foot. Park and walk west on this blocked road 300 yards, cross the old bridge, and immediately turn right onto a trail which is just above the fallen trees at the waters edge. Follow the trail 100 yards north to the thermal area.

Source map: *Boise National Forest*.

▲
▼ *Molly's Hot Spring:* At this location volunteers use a similar maze of collection pipes but prefer a single large Mickey Mouse log and tarp pool.

Vulcan Hot Springs: **Since this photograph was taken insects have ravaged the trees and floods have washed out the steps, but the geothermal hot creek is still running, awaiting some new volunteers.**

390   VULCAN HOT SPRINGS   (see map)

● **South of Warm Lake**

Once-popular, geothermal creek pool showing signs of neglect in an insect-ravaged part of Boise National Forest. Elevation 5,600 ft. Open all year.

Natural mineral water flows out of many small bubbling springs at boiling temperatures, creating a substantial hot creek which gradually cools as it runs through the woods toward the South Fork of the Salmon River. Volunteers have built a log dam across this creek at the point where the water has cooled to approximately 105º. This dam has been partly wiped out by high-water runoff, and the one-mile trail to it is no longer maintained. The apparent local custom is clothing optional.

One mile south of Stolle Meadows there is an unmarked, unofficial camping area where the head of the trail to the springs begins. It is six miles to a Forest Service campground and 32 miles to all other services.

Directions: At the west edge of the camping area is a log footbridge built by the Corps of Engineers. Cross this bridge and follow the path across two more log bridges. It is approximately one mile to the dam and pool.

Source maps: *Boise National Forest;* USGS *Warm Lake, Idaho.*

391   SUGAH (MILE 16) HOT SPRING

● **North of Warm Lake**

A sweetie of a remote soaking pool for two, located on the edge of the South Fork of the Salmon River in Payette National Forest. Elevation 4,800 ft. Open all year.

Natural mineral water flows out of a spring at 115º and cools as it goes through makeshift pipes to the volunteer-built, rock-and-masonry pool at the river's edge. Pool temperature is controlled by diverting the hot water when not needed, and/or by adding a bucket of cold river water. The apparent local custom is clothing optional.

There are no services available on the premises. There is a campground within two miles and it is 40 miles to all other services.

Directions: From the intersection of FS 22 (paved) and FS 474 (gravel), go north on FS 474 along the South Fork of the Salmon River for 16 miles to the spring. At 1.7 miles past Poverty Flats Campground there is a small (two-car) turnout on the side of the road toward the river. Look for an unmarked, steep path down to the pool.

Sourcemaps: *Payette National Forest; Boise National Forest.*

144

▲ *Sugah Hot Springs:* Hot water had to be piped in to this ideal pool location.

145 IDAHO

392   WHITE LICKS HOT SPRINGS
(see map)

● **West of Donnelly**

A large, geothermal seep serving two small bathhouses in an unofficial camping area at a wooded site surrounded by Payette National Forest. Elevation 4,800 ft. Open all year.

Natural mineral water flows out of many small springs at temperatures up to 120º, supplying two small, wood shacks, each containing a cement tub. Each tub is served by two pipes, one bringing in 110º water, the other bringing in 80º water. The tub temperature is controlled by plugging up the pipe bringing in the water not desired. Soakers are expected to drain the tub after each use. Bathing suits are not required inside the bathhouses.

A picnic area and camping are available on the premises. It is 16 miles to all other services.

Directions: From ID 55 in Donnelly, follow signs west toward Rainbow Point Campground. After crossing the bridge across Cascade Reservoir, follow FS 186 (gravel) as it starts north, curves west and then goes south. Watch for hot spring on the west side of FS 186, 3 1/2 miles south of the intersection of FS 245 and FS 186.

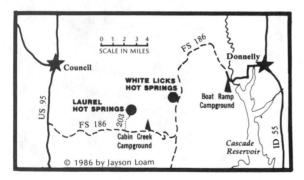

▲ *Laurel Hot Springs:* This is more than an hot spring; it is an ideal hot creek, cooling as it flows through the woods.

393   LAUREL HOT SPRINGS   (see map)

● **East of the town of Council**

Several primitive, thermal springs in a wooded canyon at the end of a rugged, two-mile hike in Payette National Forest. Elevation 4,300 ft. Open all year.

Natural mineral water flows out of several springs at temperatures up to 120º and into progressively cooler, volunteer-built soaking pools along the bottom of Warm Springs Creek. The local custom is clothing optional

There are no services available on the premises. It is two miles to a campground and 23 miles to all other services.

Directions: From Cabin Creek Campground on FS 186, go two miles west to Warm Springs Creek. Follow trail number 203 two miles north to Springs. Water is very hot where the trail crosses the creek.

Source map: *Payette National Forest.*

Krigbaum Hot Springs: This private-property hot spring soaking pool goes through cycles of being destroyed by vandals and restored by volunteers. On a fairly good day it looks like this.

Waterhole Lodge: In winter these tubs are almost better than the real thing; the doors may be closed for cozy soaking.

394 WATERHOLE LODGE

P.O. Box 37   (208) 634-7758
Lake Fork, ID 83635   PR+MH+CRV

Newly remodeled tavern, lodge and unique hot tubs with a view of the mountains. Located five miles south of McCall.

Private-space hot pools using bromine-treated tap water are for rent to the public by the hour. There are six redwood hydrojet tubs in covered patios with one side that opens toward a mountain view. Pool temperatures range from 102-106º. Each unit has an inside, heated dressing room.

A cafe, tavern, rooms and overnight camping are available on the premises. A store and service station are within five blocks, and RV hookups are within five miles. Visa and MasterCard are accepted. Phone for rates, reservations and directions.

395 KRIGBAUM HOT SPRINGS

● **East of the town of Meadows**

Primitive hot springs and soaking pool on the east bank of Goose Creek, surrounded by Payette National Forest. Elevation 4,000 ft. Open all year.

Natural mineral water flows out of a spring at 102º and is piped to a volunteer-built, rock-and-sand pool where the temperatures range from 85-95º, depending on weather conditions. The apparent local custom is clothing optional.

There are no services available on the premises. It is two miles to a store, service station, overnight camping and RV hookups, and nine miles to a motel and restaurant.

Directions: On ID 55, go one mile east from Packer Johns Cabin State Park and turn north on the gravel road along the east bank of Goose Creek. Just before the road crosses a bridge over Goose Creek, park and hike 300 yard north along the east bank to the pool.

Source map: *Payette National Forest.*

▲ *Zim's Hot Springs:* Scalding mineral water from the source pool is cooled by being sprayed into the swimming pool.

396 ZIM'S HOT SPRINGS

■ P.O. Box 314   (208) 347-9447
New Meadows, ID 83654   **PR+CRV**

Older, rural plunge and picnic grounds in an agricultural valley. Elevation 4,200 ft. Open all year.

Natural mineral water flows out of an artesian well at 151º and is cooled as it is sprayed into the chlorine-treated pools. The temperature in the outdoor swimming pool ranges from 90-100º and from 103-106º in the outdoor soaking pool. Bathing suits are required.

Locker rooms, snacks, picnic area, overnight camping and RV hookups are available on the premises. A store, service station and motel are located within four miles. Visa and MasterCard are accepted.

Directions: From the town of New Meadows, take US 95 four miles north, then follow signs to plunge.

▲ *Burgdorf Hot Springs:* This rustic resort dates back to when logs were used to build everything, including pools.

397 BURGDORF HOT SPRINGS

■   **McCall, ID 83638**   **MH**

Picturesque, mountain-rustic resort without electricity or telephone, surrounded by Payette National Forest. Elevation 6,000 ft. Open all year.

Natural mineral water flows out of a spring at 112º and directly into and through a sandy-bottom swimming pool which averages 100º and requires no chemical treatment. The pools are available only to registered guests. Bathing suits are required during the daytime.

Dressing rooms and cabins with outdoor plumbing are available on the premises.

Overnight camping is within 1/4 mile. It is 30 miles to all other services. Hiking, skiing, snowmobiling and boating are nearby. No credit cards are accepted.

Write first for reservations and information on current status and what to bring. For wintertime pick-up by snowmobile, write to the resort manager.

399 THE LODGE AT RIGGINS HOT SPRINGS

■ P.O. Box 1247   (208) 628-3785
Riggings, ID 83549   MH

Secluded 155 acre luxury resort on the banks of the Salmon River, 10 miles east of Riggins. Elevation 1,800 feet. Open all year.

Natural mineral water flows out of an artesian well at 140º and is piped to the recently remodeled soaking pool and enclosed spa. Water temperature in the flow-though spa is maintained at 105º-108º without chlorination. Water temperature in the flow-through pool is maintained at 92º-97º with a minimum of chlorination. The pools are open only to registered guests. Bathing suits are required.

Rooms with private baths are available in the main lodge and in a new three unit cabin. A stocked trout pond, a bathhouse with game room, and access to the Salmon River are available on the premises. Whitewater rafting, steelhead fishing, jetboat excursions and horses are available nearby. Via and MasterCard are accepted.

Phone for rates, reservations and directions.

The Lodge at Riggins Hot Springs: These modern tiled pools are part of the urban luxury offered by this resort on the banks of the famous River of No Return.

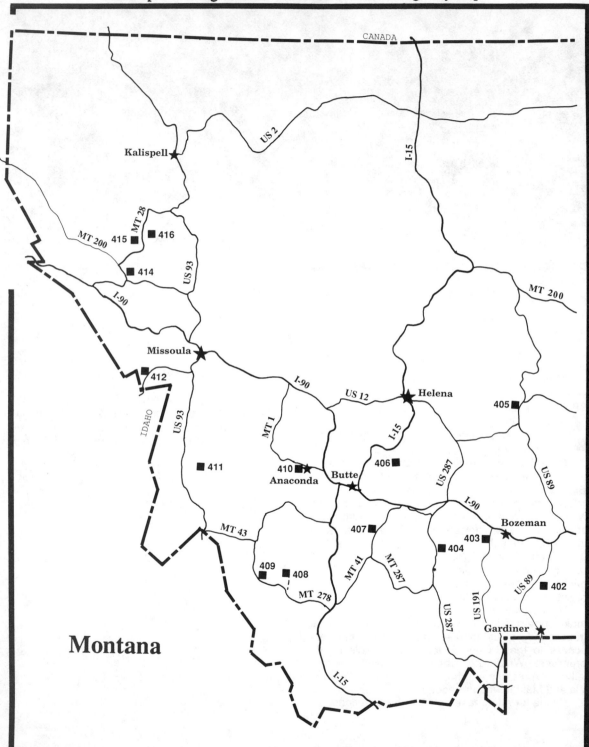

Montana

Chico Hot Springs: This all-year resort near Yellowstone National Park offers public pools full of pure mineral water, a luxury not available in the Park.

402   CHICO HOT SPRINGS

■

P.O. Box 127   (406) 333-4933

Pray, MT 59065   PR+MH

Large, older resort surrounded by Gallatin National Forest. Elevation 5,000 ft. Open all year.

Natural mineral water flows out of several springs at 118º. The outdoor swimming pool is maintained at 98º, the covered soaking pool at 105º, and one private-space hot tub at 105º. All pools operate on a flow-through basis so that no chemical treatment is needed. Pools are available to the public as well as to registered guests. Bathing suits are required except in private spaces.

Changing rooms, restaurant, saloon, hotel rooms, saddle horses, dog sled treks and a private trout lake are available on the premises. It is four miles to a store and service station and 15 miles to overnight camping and RV hookups. Visa, Discover and MasterCard are accepted.

Directions: From the town of Emigrant on US 89 south of Livingston, take MT 362 southeast for three miles. Follow signs to resort.

 Bozeman Hot Springs: Several pools with various temperatures help make this one of the most popular KOA campgrounds.

403 BOZEMAN HOT SPRINGS
81123 Gallatin Rd. **(406) 587-3030**
Bozeman, MT 59715 **PR+RV**

Tree-shaded KOA campground with mineral water pools. Elevation 4,500 ft. Open all year. Pools closed from sundown Friday to sundown Saturday.

Natural mineral water flows out of a spring at 141º and is piped to an indoor pool building. The swimming pool is maintained at 90º, and adjoining soaking pools are maintained at temperatures ranging from 100-110º. There is also a 60º cold pool. All pools operate on a flow-through basis, including cold tap water for controlling temperatures, so no chemical treatment is needed. Pools are available to the public as well as to registered guests. Bathing suits are required.

Locker rooms, grocery store, laundromat, picnic area, RV hookups and Kamper Kabins are available on the premises. It is one mile to a restaurant and service station and eight miles to a motel. Visa and MasterCard are accepted.

Location: On US 191, eight miles southwest of the town of Bozeman.

404 BEAR TRAP HOT SPRINGS
P.O. Box 2944 **(406) 685-3303**
Norris, MT 59745 **PR+CRV**

Small RV park in foothills below Tobacco Root Mountains. Elevation 5,000 ft. Open all year.

Natural mineral water flows out of artesian springs at 128º. The outdoor soaking pool is maintained at 101º in the summer and 106º in the winter. The water contains no sulfur, and no chemical treatment is added because the pool operates on a flow-through basis. The pool is available to the public as well as to registered guests. Bathing suits are required.

A store, picnic area, overnight camping and RV hookups are available on the premises. It is 1/4 mile to a cafe and service station and ten miles to a motel. No credit cards are accepted.

Directions: From US 287 in the town of Norris, go 1/4 mile east on MT 84.

Bear Trap Hot Springs: Hot artesian well water pressure supplies this cooling-tower effect 24 hours per day.

152

> *Barkell's Hot Springs Supper Club and Lounge:* This community social center combines a swimming pool, bar and restaurant in one large building.

405 SPA MOTEL

P.O. Box 370   (406) 547-3366
White Sulphur Springs, MT 59645

PR+MH

Remodeled, older resort at the foot of the Castle Mountains. Elevation 5,100. Open all year.

Natural mineral water flows out of a spring at 120º and is piped to two pools which operate on a flow-through basis, requiring no chemical treatment. The outdoor swimming pool is maintained at 94º in the summer and 102º in the winter. The indoor soaking pool is maintained at 106-108º. Bathing suits are required.

Rooms and a picnic area are available on the premises. It is less that five blocks to all other services. Visa and MasterCard are accepted.

Location: On US 89 at the west end of White Sulphur Springs.

406 BOULDER HOT SPRINGS

P.O. Box 457   (406) 225-4339
Boulder, MT 59632   **PR+MH**

Large historic resort in the process of being remodeled. Located at the foot of the Elkhorn Mountains. Elevation 5,000 feet. Open all year.

Natural mineral water flows out of several springs at temperatures of 150º to 175º and is piped to indoor and outdoor pools. The flow-through soaking pools in the men's and women's bathhouses are maintained at 104º. The other indoor pool is maintained at 76º. All of the indoor pools are drained and filled each day, eliminating the need for chemical treatment of the water. The outdoor pool is treated with chlorine and the temperature will vary with the seasons. Bathing suits are not required in the bathhouses.

Overnight accomodations, including meals, are available for groups. Future plans include bed & breakfast service for individuals. Phone for status of construction. Massage is available on the premises. No credit cards are accepted.

Phone for rates, reservations and directions.

407 BARKELL'S HOT SPRINGS SUPPER CLUB AND LOUNGE

(406) 287-3606
Silver Star, MT 59751   **PR**

Community plunge with adjoining bar and restaurant. Elevation 4,500 ft. Open all year.

Natural mineral water flows out of a spring at 180º into a cooling pond. It is then piped to an indoor swimming pool maintained at a temperature of 75-100º by the addition of cold tap water as needed. The pool is drained and refilled weekly so that no chemical treatment is needed. Bathing suits are required.

A store, service station, overnight camping and RV hookups are located within one mile. It is 10 miles to a motel. Visa and MasterCard are accepted.

Location: On MT 41 between Twin Bridges and Whitehall, 1/4 mile south of the town of Silver Star.

408   ELKHORN HOT SPRINGS
P.O. Box 514   **(800) 722-8978**
Polaris, MT 59746   **PR+MH+C**

Beautifully restored mountain resort, lodge and rustic cabins, situated among the tall trees of Elkhorn National Forest. Elevation 7,300 ft. Open all year.

Natural mineral water flows out of six springs with temperatures ranging from 106-140º. The outdoor swimming pool is maintained at 88-95º and the outdoor soaking pool at 95-104º. There are two coed Roman saunas maintained at 110º. All pools are drained and refilled weekly so that no chemical treatment is needed. Pools are available to the public as well as to registered guests. Bathing suits are required.

Dressing rooms, cafe, tent spaces, picnic area, overnight camping and cabins are available on the premises. Hunting, fishing, backpacking, rock and mineral hunting, skiing and snowmobile trails are available nearby. Pick-up service is provided from the city of Butte by prior arrangement. Visa and MasterCard are accepted.

Directions: From I-15, three miles south of Dillon, take MT 278 west 27 miles to large sign, turn north, and follow gravel road 13 miles to resort.

◄
▼ *Elkhorn Hot Springs:* These chlorine-free pools are a welcome sight after a day of summer hiking or winter snowmobiling.

▲ *Fairmont Hot Springs:* This destination resort is a modern spin-off from the popular historic spa in British Columbia.

409   JACKSON HOT SPRINGS
■
P.O. Box 808   (406) 834-3151
Jackson, MT 59736   PR+MH+CRV

Renovated lodge and cabins on the main street of a small town. Elevation 6,400 ft. Open all year.

Natural mineral water flows out of a spring at 137º and is piped to cabins and an indoor pool. The indoor swimming pool is maintained at 98-100º and operates on a flow-through basis, so no chemical treatment is necessary. Water temperatures in cabin bathtubs may be controlled by adding cold tap water as needed. The swimming pool is available to the public as well as to registered guests. Bathing suits are required.

Dressing rooms, restaurant, cabins, overnight camping and RV hookups are available on the premises. It is one block to a store and service station. Visa and MasterCard are accepted.

Location: On MT 278 in the town of Jackson.

410   FAIRMONT HOT SPRINGS
■
1500 Fairmont Rd.   (406) 797-3241
Anaconda, MT 59711   PR+MH

Large hotel-type resort and real-estate development in a wide valley. Elevation 5,300. Open all year.

Natural mineral water flows out of a spring at 160º and is piped to an enclosed water slide and a group of pools where it is treated with chlorine. The indoor and outdoor swimming pools are maintained at 80-85º and the indoor and outdoor soaking pools at 105º. There are also men's and women's steam rooms. Facilities are available to the public as well as to registered guests. Bathing suits are required.

Locker rooms, restaurant, lounge, rooms, mini-zoo, tennis, golf course and horseback riding are available on the premises. Overnight camping, RV hookups, country store and service station are one block away. Visa, MasterCard, Discover and American Express are accepted.

Directions: From I-90, 12 miles west of Butte, take the Gregson-Fairmont exit (#211) and follow signs to the resort.

411   SLEEPING CHILD HOT SPRINGS

P.O. Box 768   **(406) 363-6250**

■ **Hamilton, MT 59840**   **PR+MH**

A small resort designed to provide day use "rustic elegance," surrounded by Bitterroot National Forest. Elevation 5,400 ft. Closed January and February.

Natural mineral water flows out of a spring at 125° and is piped to two outdoor soaking pools and one large outdoor swimming pool. The swimming pool is temperature is maintained at $90-97^\circ$, and the soaking pools are maintained at 106° and 112°. All pools are flow-through, so no chemical treatment is needed. Bathing suits are required.

No rooms for rent and no overnight camping. Locker rooms, bar and restaurant are available on the premises, but may be closed some days of the week. Phone ahead for current information. A store, service station and RV hookups are located within 15 miles. Visa and MasterCard are accepted.

Directions: From the town of Hamilton, take US 93 south to MT 38, then go east to MT 501. Follow signs to resort. The last five miles are on gravel road.

▲
►
Sleeping Child Hot Springs: This location no longer offers overnight accomodations but the restaurant and bar are only a few steps from the pools.

156

412   LOLO HOT SPRINGS RESORT

■   38500 Highway 12   (406) 273-2290
       Lolo, MT 59847   PR+MH+CRV

An historic resort being restored and expanded in a spectacular mountain setting 30 miles west of Missoula. Elevation 4,700 ft. Open all year.

Natural mineral water flows out of two springs at temperatures of 110º and 117º and is piped to two pools. The large outdoor pool maintains a temperature of 92º with a continuous flow-through system that requires a minimum of chlorination. The covered soaking pool maintains a temperature of 103-105º on a continuous flow-through basis that requires no chemical treatment of the water. Bathing suits are required.

Facilities include dressing rooms, bathhouse, RV park, campground and picnic area, open 5/1 thru 10/1. New full restaurant, motel and bar open year round. Visa and MasterCard accepted. All other services are available in Missoula. Phone for rates and reservations.

Location: On US 12, 25 miles west of Lolo.

▲ Giant boulders near the *Lolo Hot Springs* pool serve as sun-decks-with-a-view.

▲ *Lolo Hot Springs Resort:* This indoor soaking pool operates on a flow-through basis so it is chlorine-free.

▲ *Quinn's Paradise Resort:* Recreational use
of mineral water, rather than medicinal
use, is a key theme at this resort.

414   QUINN'S PARADISE RESORT: A NATURAL HOT SPRINGS

■ P.O. Box 219   (406) 826-3150
Paradise, MT 59856   PR+MH+CRV

Complete family resort on the banks of the Clark Fork River. Elevation 2,700 ft. Open all year.

Natural mineral water flows out of a spring at 120º. The outdoor swimming pool is treated with chlorine and maintained at a temperature of 88º. The outdoor hydrojet pool is maintained at 100º and operates on a flow-through basis so that no chemical treatment of the water is needed. There are two indoor, private-space fiberglass tubs in which the water temperature can be controlled by the customer. These pools are drained and refilled after each use, so that no chemical treatment is necessary. Pools are available to the public as well as to registered guests. Bathing suits are required except in private spaces.

Dressing rooms, cafe, bar, store, service station, rooms and cabins, overnight camping, RV hookups and fishing are available on the premises. Visa and MasterCard are accepted.

Location: On MT 135, three miles south of the junction with MT 200, which is east of St. Regis.

415 SYMES HOTEL AND MEDICINAL SPRINGS

Hot Springs, MT 59845
(406) 741-2361
PR+MH

Historic hotel with a long tradition of mineral water and other health treatments. Elevation 2,900 ft. Open all year.

Natural mineral water flows out of an artesian well at 80-90º and is heated as needed for use in soaking tubs. There are nine individual soaking tubs in the men's bathhouse and six in the women's bathhouse. There are also hotel rooms with mineral water piped to the room. Temperature is controllable within each tub, and no chemical treatment is added. Bathhouses are available to the public as well as to registered guests.

Locker rooms, hotel rooms and chiropractic services are available on the premises. It is two blocks to a cafe, store and service station and six blocks to overnight camping and RV hookups. No credit cards are accepted.

Directions: From MT 382 northeast of St. Regis, follow signs to the town of Hot Springs and then to the hotel.

416 CAMP AQUA

P.O. Box K
Hot Springs, MT 59845
(406) 741-3480
PR+MH+CRV

Well-maintained, family rent-a-tub establishment with overnight facilities surrounded by rolling foothills. Elevation 2,750 ft. Open all year.

Natural mineral water flows out of an artesian well at 124º and is piped to the bathhouse building. There are six large indoor soaking pools in private rooms, each with steam bath, sauna, shower and toilet. Pool water temperature is controllable by each customer up to 110º. The pools are scrubbed down frequently, so no chemical treatment is needed. Bathing suits are not required in private rooms. Geothermal heat is used in all buildings.

Cabins, picnic area, overnight camping and RV hookups are available on the premises. It is six miles to all other services. No credit cards are accepted.

Directions: From MT 28, 2 1/2 miles north of Hot Springs junction, follow signs two miles east on gravel road to resort.

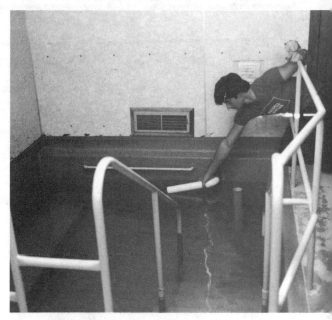

Camp Aqua: The soaking pools in these private-space rooms were built large enough to hold a whole group or family.

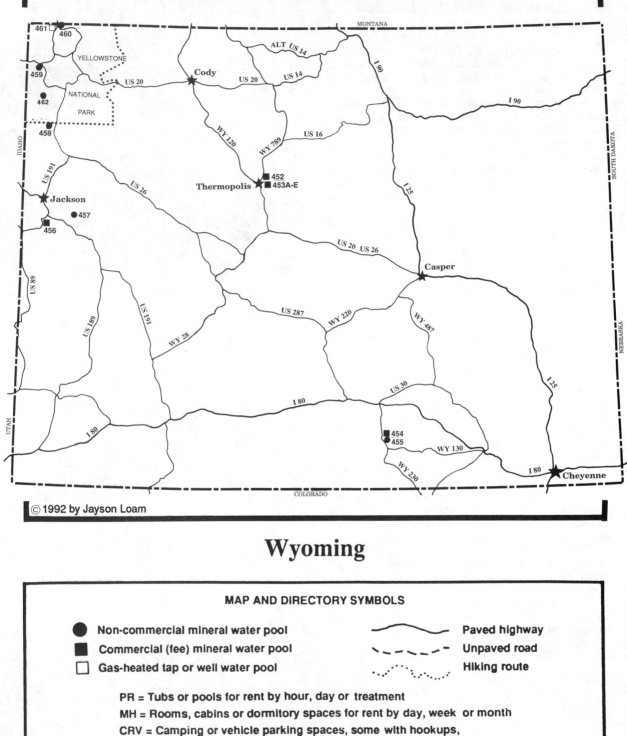

© 1992 by Jayson Loam

Wyoming

MAP AND DIRECTORY SYMBOLS

● Non-commercial mineral water pool

■ Commercial (fee) mineral water pool

□ Gas-heated tap or well water pool

〜〜〜 Paved highway

- - - Unpaved road

········ Hiking route

PR = Tubs or pools for rent by hour, day or treatment

MH = Rooms, cabins or dormitory spaces for rent by day, week or month

CRV = Camping or vehicle parking spaces, some with hookups,
for rent by day, week, month or year

▲ *Fountain Of Youth:* A portion of the Sacajawea Well output flows into a cooling pond (foreground) and then on into the very large swimming pool.

It is probable that this well taps the same underground hot mineral water reservoir as that which supplies the Big Spring in Thermopolis, two miles away.

452   FOUNTAIN OF YOUTH

■ P.O. Box 711   (307) 864-3265
Thermopolis, WY 82443   PR+CRV

Well-kept RV park featuring a unique, large soaking pool. Elevation 4,300 ft. Open all year.

Natural mineral water flows out of the historic Sacajawea Well at the rate of over one million gallons per day. Some of this 130º water is channeled through a cooling pond into a 200-foot-long soaking pool where the temperature varies from 104º at the inflow end to 99º at the outflow. The pool is available only to registered day campers and overnight campers. Bathing suits are required.

Restrooms, showers, overnight camping and RV hookups are available on the premises. It is two miles to all other services. No credit cards are accepted.

Location: On US 20, two miles north of the town of Thermopolis.

This square mile of land, with the Big Spring in the center, was presented to the State of Wyoming by the Federal Government after it had been purchased from the Shoshone and Arapahoe Indians in 1896. Elevation 4,300 feet. Open all year.

All of the establishments on the grounds are supplied with natural mineral water from the Big Spring, which flows out of the ground at 135 degrees. Walkways have been provided through the large tufa terraces which have been built up by mineral deposits from the spring over the centuries. Facilities provided include a large tree-shaded picnic area in the center of the grounds.

All services not provided by an establishment within the State Park are available within 1/2 mile in the city of Thermopolis.

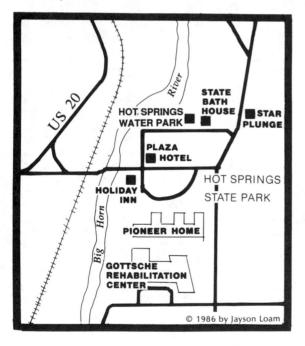

© 1986 by Jayson Loam

453A   HOT SPRINGS WATER PARK
(see map)
P.O. Box 750   (307) 864-9250
Thermopolis, WY 82443   PR

The outdoor and indoor swimming pools are maintained at 85-95º year-round, and the indoor soaking pool is maintained at 104º. The indoor steambath is maintained at 110-115º. All pools operate on a flow-through basis, so no chemical treatment is needed. Bathing suits are required.

Locker rooms and snack bar are available on the premises. Visa and MasterCard are accepted.

453B   STATE BATH HOUSE   (see map)
State Park   (307) 864-3765
Thermopolis, WY 82443 noncommercial

The outdoor and indoor soaking pools are maintained at 104º. The temperature in 16 (eight men's and eight women's) individual soaking tubs is adjustable by the person using the tub. All pools use non-chlorinated, flow-through mineral water. No charge is made for pool or tub use.

Changing rooms are available and bathing suits are required in the communal pools. There is a nominal charge for renting suits or towels. No credit cards are accepted.

 State Bath House: Sparkling clean no-charge pools, indoor and outdoor, are popular with seniors. The Big Spring tufa mounds are located a few yards away.

453C STAR PLUNGE (see map)
P.O. Box 627 (307) 864-3771
Thermopolis, WY 82443 PR

The outdoor swimming pool is maintained at 92-96º and the indoor swimming pool is maintained at 96-98º. The hot pool also has a hydrojet section which is maintained at 104º. Included are an indoor and an outdoor waterslide which are open throughout the year. The coed steambath is maintained at 118º. All pools are flow-through requiring no chemical treatment. Bathing suits are required.

Locker rooms and snack bar are available on the premises. No credit cards are accepted.

▲ *Star Plunge:* 105º water continuously overflows from the small pool.

▶ *Holiday Inn:* Eight private-space indoor pools supplement these outdoor pools.

453D PLAZA HOTEL AND APARTMENTS
(see map)
P.O. Box 671 (307) 864-2251
Thermopolis, WY 82443 PR+MH

An older resort building with men's and women's bathhouses. Each bathhouse has four individual mineral-water tubs and two steambaths. Bathing suits are not required in bathhouses.

Hotel rooms, massage and sweat wraps are available on the premises. Visa and MasterCard are accepted.

453E HOLIDAY INN (see map)
P.O. Box 1323 (307) 864-3131
Thermopolis, WY 82443 PR+MH

Conventional, major hotel with a unique adaptation of men's and women's bathhouses. Each bathhouse has private spaces for four individual soaking tubs, two saunas and two steambaths. The private spaces are rented to couples, even though they are in the men's and women's bathhouses.

The indoor soaking tubs are temperature controllable up to 110º, use natural mineral water, and are drained after each use so that no chemical treatment is needed. The outdoor hydrojet pool also uses natural mineral water without chemical treatment and is maintained at a temperature of 104º. The outdoor swimming pool uses gas-heated, chlorine-treated tap water and is maintained at a temperature of 81-84º. There is also a private indoor hydropool. All pools and the athletic club facilities are available to the public as well as to registered guests. Bathing suits are required in all outdoor public areas.

Restaurant and hotel rooms are available on the premises. Visa, MasterCard, American Express and Carte Blanche are accepted.

454 THE SARATOGA INN

P.O. Box 869   (307) 326-5261
Saratoga, WY 82331   MH

Modest golf and tennis resort surrounded by rolling ranch country. Elevation 6,800 ft. Open April 1 thru October.

Natural mineral water is pumped out of a spring at 114º and piped to an outdoor swimming pool which is treated with chlorine and maintained at 100º. An outdoor, rock soaking pool is built over another spring and is maintained at 100-105º, with chlorine added as needed. Pool use is reserved for registered guests. Bathing suits are required.

Hotel rooms, RV hookups, restaurant, lounge, golf and tennis are available on the premises. It is four blocks to a store and service station and one mile to overnight camping. Visa, MasterCard, Diners and American Express are accepted.

Directions: From WY 130 in the town of Saratoga, go east on Bridge St. and follow signs four blocks to the resort.

Hobo Pool: When the town built a fenced swimming pool it respected hobos by also building an adjoining free pool.

455 HOBO POOL

In the town of Saratoga

An improved but unfenced soaking pool and a fenced municipal swimming pool located on the banks of the North Platte River. Elevation 6,800 ft. Open all year.

Natural mineral water flows out of the source spring at 115º. A large cement soaking pool (free to the public) maintains a temperature of 100-110º. Volunteers have channeled the soaking pool run-off into shallow rock pools along the edge of the river. A daily charge is made for the use of the swimming pool, which is maintained at 90º. Bathing suits are required.

There are showers and public rest rooms on the premises. It is three blocks to all services. No credit cards are accepted.

Directions: On WY 130 in the town of Saratoga, watch for HOBO POOL sign, then follow signs four blocks east to the pool.

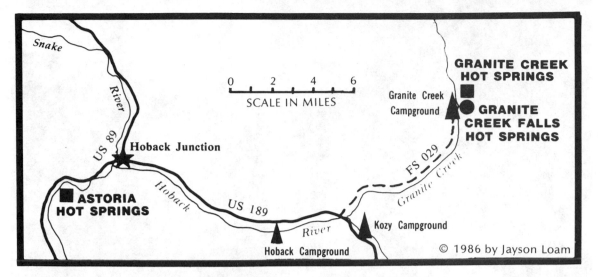

> **Astoria Mineral Hot Springs:** The pool and lawn area at this popular summer resort for RVs has a sweeping view of the Snake River gateway to the Teton Mountains.

---

456   ASTORIA MINERAL HOT SPRINGS
(see map)

Star Route, Box 18   (307) 733-2659
Jackson, WY 83001   PR+CRV

Large, well-kept RV resort on the south bank of the Snake River. Elevation 6,100 ft. Open mid-May to mid-September.

Natural mineral water flows out of a spring at 104º and is piped to an outdoor swimming pool which is treated with chlorine and maintained at a temperature of 84º-92º. The pool is available to the public as well as to registered guests. Bathing suits are required.

Locker rooms, picnic area, volleyball, basketball, tent spaces, RV hookups, grocery store, and river raft trips are available on the premises. It is two miles to a cafe, service station and motel. No credit cards are accepted.

Location: On US 26, 17 miles south of the town of Jackson.

▲ *Granite Creek Hot Springs:* For those who like mountains streams and camping in the woods, but prefer to soak in a supervised hot pool, this is the place.

GRANITE HOT SPRINGS SWIMMING POOL

OPERATED UNDER SPECIAL USE PERMIT
BRIDGER·TETON NATIONAL FOREST

POOL CONSTRUCTED IN 1933 BY
CIVILIAN CONSERVATION CORPS (CCC)

AVERAGE YEARLY   WATER TEMP.
SNOWFALL 400"   SUMMER 93°
ELEVATION 6987   WINTER 112°

457 GRANITE CREEK HOT SPRINGS
(see map on preceding page)

● **East of Hoback Junction**   **PR**

Part of a major bonanza for lovers of natural beauty and natural mineral water. Elevation 7,000 ft. Open all year, including the winter season for those who have snow cats.

Natural mineral water flows out of a spring at 112° and tumbles directly into a large cement pool built by the CCC in the 1930's. Cold stream water is added as needed to maintain the pool temperature of 95° in the summer and 105° in the winter. The pool is drained and refilled each day, so no chemical treatment is needed. Bathing suits are required.

Changing rooms and rest rooms are available on the premises, which is operated under a lease with the Forest Service. The site is closed and gates are locked from 8 P.M. to 10 A.M. A large, wooded, creekside campground is one-half mile away. It is ten miles to a cafe and motel and 22 miles to all other services.

Fifteen minutes by trail from this site is Granite Creek Falls Hot Spring. Natural mineral water flows out of a creek bank immediately below the falls at 130° and meanders through creekbed rocks where volunteers have built soaking pools in which the hot and cold waters mix. These rock-and-sand pools must be rebuilt after each annual high-water washout. Although the spring is partly visible from the road, the apparent local custom is clothing optional.

Allow no less than one full day and night to enjoy these two hot springs, the campground, and the beautiful scenery of Granite Creek Valley.

▲ *Granite Creek Falls Hot Spring:* Do not attempt to reach this spring by fording Granite Creek. Go to the *Granite Creek Hot Spring* pool and then use the trail.

▲ The pool at *Granite Creek Hot Springs* remains open during the winter for skiers and snowmobilers who want out of the snow and into a warm geothermal soak.

458   HUCKLEBERRY HOT SPRINGS
(see map)

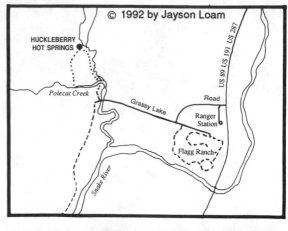

    North of the town of Jackson

Large group of primitive hot springs along the north bank of Polecat Creek, within Grand Teton National Park, near the south entrance to Yellowstone National Park. Elevation 6,800 ft. Open all year.

Natural mineral water flows out of many springs at temperatures up to 130º, cooling as it follows various channels to the creek. Volunteers have built small rock-and-mud soaking pools at several places where the water is in the 100-105º range. There are very few visitors so the apparent local custom is clothing optional. However, it is advisable to have a bathing suit handy in case anyone objects to skinnydippers.

There are no services available on the premises. There is a commercial campground within one mile, and all other services are within five miles.

During the 1980s the Forest Service transferred the administration of this area to Grand Teton National Park. The Park Service then demolished the existing franchise campground at Huckleberry Hot springs for the announced purpose of "returning the area to its natural state." This action included bulldozing the swimming pool and removing the access bridge over Polecat Creek. Now it is necessary to wade Polecat Creek in order to get to the springs from the parking area at the end of the old access road. Huckleberry Hot Springs is not shown on the Grand Teton National Park map and trails in the area are not maintained.

There is an official warning sign (see photo) which makes it clear that soaking in the pools is permitted "at your own risk." This sign implies that one or more people have contracted meningitis during the last 30 years from naegleria fowleri in the old swimming pool or in the soaking pools. However, the U.S. Public Health Service does not have even one recorded case. Furthermore, naegleri fowleri has never been found in any of the official tests of the water in Huckleberry Hot Springs.

Source map: USGS *Flagg Ranch*. (hot springs not shown on Grand Teton National Park map)

Huckleberry Hot Springs: This is the USE AT YOUR OWN RISK sign which greets visitors walking toward the springs.

This is the pool and campground which was operated by the Forest Service until the early 1980s, when the Park Service took over and bulldozed it all away.

▲ As the main runoff from *Huckleberry Hot Springs* flows toward Polecat Creek it forms shallow warm soaking pools.

▲ Runoff from one of the main springs supplies a natural hot showerbath as it falls into a shallow soaking pool.

▲ Water from another spring flows in the opposite direction to this soaking pool on an upstream portion of Polecat Creek.

Madison Campground Warm Spring:
Geothermal water combines with river water as it percolates up through the mud, so people may legally sit in it.

459   MADISON CAMPGROUND WARM SPRING

In Yellowstone National Park

Shallow, mud-bottom ditch near a campground inside the west boundary of Yellowstone National Park. Elevation 6,800 ft. Open all year.

Natural mineral water combined with underground river water bubbles up through a mud flat on the north bank of the Firehole River, just south of the campground. Volunteers have built a small sod dam across a narrow channel in order to accumulate enough 100° water to be 18 inches deep. (The chief ranger wants it known that those volunteers were breaking officially posted park regulations when they built that dam and that anyone caught in the act will be cited and prosecuted.) Bathing suits are required.

No services, other than the campground, are available at the springs. Refer to the NPS Yellowstone Park map for the location of all services.

Directions: Park on Loop G in Madison Campground and walk 100 yards south toward the Firehole River.

460   BOILING RIVER

● **In Yellowstone National Park**

Turbulent confluence of hot mineral water and cold river water along the west bank of the Gardiner River, just below Park Headquarters at Mammoth Hot Spring. Elevation 5,500 ft. Open all year during daylight hours only.

Natural mineral water flows out of a very large spring at 140º and travels 30 yards through an open channel where it tumbles down the south bank of the Gardiner River. Volunteers have rearranged some rocks in the river to control the flow of cold water in an eddy pocket where the hot and cold water churn into a swirling mixture which varies from 50º-110º. (The chief ranger wants it known that those volunteers were breaking officially posted Park regulations when they rearranged the rocks in the river, and that anyone caught in the act will be cited and prosecuted). Bathing suits are required.

No services are available at this location. Refer to the NPS Yellowstone Park map for the location of all services.

Directions: On the North Entrance Road between Mammoth Hot Spring and the town of Gardiner, look for the 45th Parallel sign on the east side of the road. Turn into the parking lot behind that sign and hike 1/2 mile upstream to where Boiling River cascades over the riverbank.

▲ *Boiling River:* When the scalding water from Boiling River spring falls into the cold river, people may legally get in it.

▲ This is not a relaxed soak in a quiet pool, but rather a stimulating challenge to remain standing in the turbulence.

461 MAMMOTH HOT SPRINGS HOTEL AND CABINS

Mammoth Hot Springs   (307) 344-7311
☐   Yellowstone National Park, WY 82190

Four fiberglass, hydrojet pools filled with chlorinated, electrically heated tap water behind high board fences adjoining four small cabins. Elevation 6,200 ft. Open all year.

These pools are rented for public use by the hour during the winter. During the summer they are for the private use of the registered guests in each of the four cabins. Phone for rates and reservations.

462 SHOSHONE GEYSER BASIN

●   **In Yellowstone National Park**

Several primitive creek-side soaking pools along a beautiful nine-mile trail from Kepler Cascades to the west end of Shoshone Lake. Elevation 7,900 feet.

Boiling hot natural mineral water erupts from geyser cones and bubbles out of hot springs, flowing to join nearby cold streams. Rocks and sand have been arranged by volunteers to make small shallow pools where the two waters combine at tempertures tolerable by human skin. The apparent local custom is clothing-optional.

There are no services at this location. However, there are several campgrounds in the Shoshone Lake and Shoshone Creek area, for which camping permits are required.

The trail begins 100 yards up the road from Kepler Cascades, a 2.7 mile drive southeast from the Old Faithful overpass. If you do not already have hiking guides and/or detailed maps of the area, obtain them when you apply for a camping permit. At that time, also ask about weather conditions and any other pertinent information.

▲ *Shoshone Geyser Basin:* This is one of the more remote legal soaking pools where geothermal water joins a surface stream.

▲ *Mammoth Hot Springs Hotel:* This pool of chlorinated tap water looks like an ordinary rent-a-tub in any big city.

IN YELLOWSTONE'S
THERMAL AREAS
IT IS UNLAWFUL TO

TRAVEL OFF BOARDWALKS OR TRAILS
TAKE PETS ON BOARDWALKS OR TRAILS
THROW OBJECTS INTO POOLS OR GEYSERS
MARK THERMAL FEATURES
BATHE IN THERMAL POOLS OR STREAMS.

▲ This legal swimming fun at Midway Bridge was banned in 1979 for being too distracting.

STONE WALL AT YELLOWSTONE

Fourteen years ago, when I started the field research for my hot spring guides, I looked forward to soaking in the abundance of geothermal water in Olympic National Park in Washington, in Hot Springs National Park in Arkansas, and especially in Yellowstone National Park in Wyoming.

Olympic National Park actually has several primitive out-in-the-woods hot springs with volunteer-built soaking pools available to the pubic, and also has commercial cement-and-tile mineral water hot pools at Sol Duc Resort. In Arkansaas, all the springs have been capped but the hot mineral water is piped to numerous public bathhouses and hotels in the Park and in the adjoining town. By vivid contrast, the official policy of Yellowstone National Park management is to discourage any form of bathing in geothermal water.

An official Yellowstone National Park regulation prohibits bathing in, or other use of, all geothermal springs, and their run-off streams, until after the geothermal water has mixed with surface water in a creek or river. Therefore, soaking in any spring is illegal and volunteers are not permitted to build rock-and-sand soaking pools where run-off streams have cooled to tolerable temperatures.

There are just four places in the Park where a legal mix of hot geothermal water and cold river water is practical for human use:
1. Madison Campground Warm Spring.
2. Boiling River.
3. Shoshone Geyser Basin
4. Firehole River at Midway Geyser Basin Bridge.
Although Midway was (and is) a legal geothermal and surface water mix, the Park Service arbitrarily banned human use in 1979 on the grounds that the bathers were "too much of a distraction."

Madison Campground and Boiling River do not appear on the Yellowstone National Park map, or in the official literature supplied to all visitors. Those two locations are not mentioned on signs along nearby roads, they are not served by maintained trails, and there are no guidance signs pointing the way from any parking area. The Park Service has deliberately chosen not to help visitors find the only two convenient places where they can legally soak in hot mineral water.

When I inquired at Old Faithful Inn about the availability of hot tubs or hot pools for hotel guests, I was informed that the only place in the Park with such facilities was the Hotel at Mammoth Hot Springs. (see preceding page) The thought of soaking in a plastic pool of tap water, heated by electricity, behind a high board fence, did not even come close to my expectation of enjoying the natural beauty and mineral water of Yellowstone National Park.

I do understand that the Mammoth Hot Springs Hotel operators had to build some kind, any kind, of hot pools in order to compete with the other major commercial resorts in the Rocky Mountains. However, I do not understand a Park Service policy which permits such artificial and inefficient construction while allowing thousand of gallons per minute of natural hot mineral water to waste from Boiling River into the Gardiner River only a thousand yards away from the hotel.

It is my unpleasant duty to report that Yellowstone National Park management chooses to ignore the desire of leg-weary visitors to relax in a safe and legal hot mineral water soak, and that any suggestion that the Park Service should reconsider this policy is met with a blunt official stone wall.

Jayson Loam

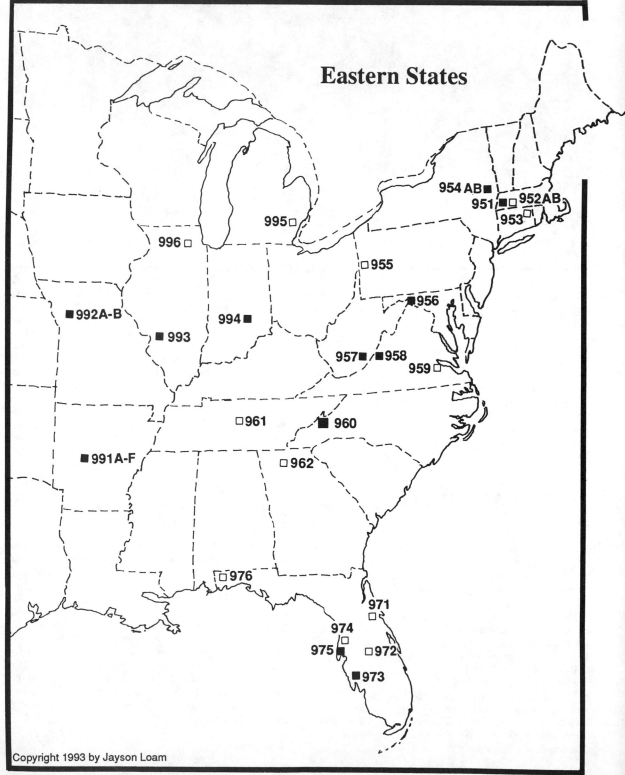

Eastern States

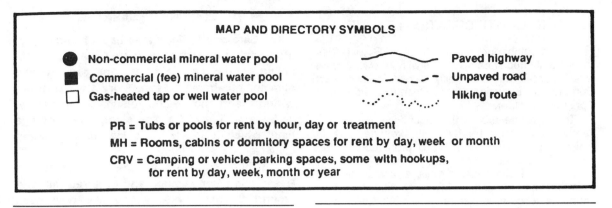

MAP AND DIRECTORY SYMBOLS

● Non-commercial mineral water pool

■ Commercial (fee) mineral water pool

☐ Gas-heated tap or well water pool

〰 Paved highway

- - - - - Unpaved road

⋯⋯⋯ Hiking route

PR = Tubs or pools for rent by hour, day or treatment

MH = Rooms, cabins or dormitory spaces for rent by day, week or month

CRV = Camping or vehicle parking spaces, some with hookups,
for rent by day, week, month or year

951   SAND SPRINGS POOL
■   Sand Springs Road   (413) 458-5205
   Williamstown, MA 01267

An historic seasonal plunge located in the heart of the Berkshire Hills in northwestern Massachusetts. Elevation 900 ft. Open May-September.

Natural mineral water flows out of a spring at 74º and is piped to several pools where it is gas-heated and treated with chlorine. The whirlpool is maintained at a temperature of 102º. The swimming pool and toddler's pool are maintained at approximately 80º. Bathing suits are required.

Facilities include changing rooms, sundeck, exercise room, sauna, snack bar, dance floor, picnic tables and large lawn. A motel, service station, restaurant and other services are available within 10 blocks. No credit cards are accepted.

Directions: From the Williamstown municipal building on US 7, drive north to Sand Springs Rd. Turn right and follow signs to pool.

952   EAST HEAVEN TUB CO.
☐   33 West St.   (413) 586-6843
   Northampton, MA 01060   PR

Beautiful, Japanese-motif rental facility located across from Smith College in the Connecticut Valley.

Private-space hot pools using gas-heated tap water treated with bromine are for rent to the public. There are four indoor tubs in private rooms and three outdoor tubs in private, roofless enclosures on the roof. All are maintained at a temperature of 104º.

Sales of saunas, hot tubs and spas are conducted on the premises. No credit cards are accepted. Phone for rates, reservations and directions.

952B   SPA OF AMHERST
☐   175ND University Drive   (413) 253-7727
   Amherst, MA 01002   PR

New rental facility located near the University of Massachusetts in central Amherst.

Private-space hot pools using gas-heated tap water treated with bromine are for rent to the public. There are four indoor private-space tubs which are maintained at temperatures of 102-104º.

Facilities include four tanning beds. Massage is available on the premises. Visa, MasterCard, American Express and Discover are accepted.

Phone for rates, reservations and directions.

◀ *East Heaven Tub Co.:* This establishment handles hot tub sales and service in addition to hourly rentals. Therefore, it offers different types of tubs for rent so that potential buyers can base their decisions on direct personal experience.

953   SOLAIR RECREATION LEAGUE

☐   P.O. Box 187   (203) 928-9174
    Southbridge, MA 01550   PR+MH+CRV

A family nudist campground with its own private lake, located on 350 hilly acres in northeast Connecticut. Elevation 600 ft. Open to visitors from April to November.

The hydrojet tub in the clubhouse uses gas-heated well water treated with bromine and is maintained at 104º. Clothing is prohibited in the pool and beach area, optional elsewhere.

Facilities include hiking trails, a private lake for swimming and boating, a clubhouse with an electric sauna, a wood-fired sauna, a shower building, a large game room, dining hall, tennis and volleyball courts, horseshoe pits and children's playground. Rental cabins, RV hook-ups and tenting spaces are available on the premises. No credit cards are accepted. It is four miles to a store and service station.

Note: This is a membership organization not open to the public for drop-in visits, but interested visitors may be issued a guest pass by prior arrangement. Telephone or write for information and directions.

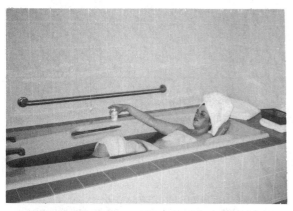

▲ *Crystal Spa:* In modern bathhouses, single-person tubs are acrylic trimmed in tile rather than claw-footed cast iron.

THE SPRINGS OF SARATOGA

The Saratoga Springs area has a two-century-old tradition of providing natural beauty, health-giving geothermal water, and the gaiety of it's summer racetrack season. More than a dozen springs and hot wells discharge naturally-carbonated mineral water along the Saratoga Fault which is located in a low basin between Lake George and Albany.

In 1909 the State of New York created a Reservation Commission and acquired the land around Geyser Creek, which has now been designated as Saratoga Spa State Park. Some geothermal activities are still accessible for public viewing, such as the only spouting geyser east of the Mississippi River.

Bathing in mineral water is available only at the Lincoln and Roosevelt bathhouses in the Park, and at the Crystal Spa bathhouse, on South Broadway, in the city of Saratoga Springs. All bathhouses have separate men's and women's sections using one-person tubs which are drained and filled after each use so that no chemical treatment of the water is necessary.

954A   ROOSEVELT BATHHOUSE

■   Saratoga Spa State Park (518) 584-2011
    Saratoga Springs, NY 12866   PR

Large, traditional state-owned bathhouse with nearby hotel and conference center operated by TW Services. Open all yeaar.

Mineral water flows out of a spring at 52º and is piped to individual tubs in private rooms. Along the way it is heated to 99º, the maximum permitted in the state-owned bathhouse.

Hot packs and massage are also available on the premises.

Credit cards are not accepted. Phone for rates, reservations and directions.

954B   CRYSTAL SPA

■   92 S. Broadway   (518) 584-2556
    Saratoga Springs, NY 12866   PR

Newly constructed privately-owned spa associated with the Grand Union Motel. Open all year.

Mineral water flows out of a spring at 52º and is piped to individual soaking tubs where it is mixed with 149º tap water as needed to obtain the desired soaking temperature.

Sauna, massage, facials, manicures and pedicures are available on the premises. No credit cards are accepted. Phone for rates, reservations and directions.

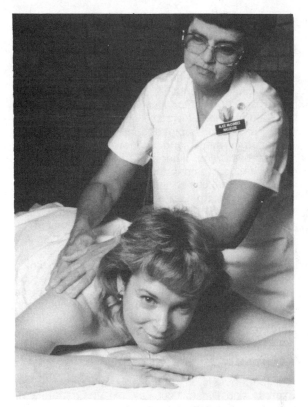

▲ *Berkeley Springs State Park:* Massage is one of the customer services offered at this state-owned hot spring enterprise.

956 BERKELEY SPRINGS STATE PARK
(304) 258-2711
■ **Berkeley Springs, WV 25411** PR

Large, traditional bathhouse and plunge operated as a state park, located in a narrow valley in West Virginia's eastern panhandle. Elevation 620 ft. Open 362 days per year.

Two thousand gallons per minute of mineral water flow out of several springs at a temperature of 74.3º. A portion of this water is steam-heated to 102º and piped to private, one-person bathtubs in the main bathhouse and to private tiled baths in the Old Roman Bath House. All are drained and refilled after each use so that no chemical treatment of the water is necessary. The Old Roman Bath House is open weekends all year, and daily from Memorial Day to Columbus Day. Mineral spring water is also piped directly to the outdoor swimming pool which is treated with chlorine and is open from Memorial Day through Labor Day.

Facilities include steam cabinets. Massage, heat treatments and other health services are available on the premises. Visa and Mastercard are accepted. All other services are available in the adjoining town of Berkeley Springs. Phone for rates, reservations and directions.

▲ The mineral water at *Berkeley Springs State Park* has to be heated an extra 30º above the source spring temperature, but the Bath House does have coed pools.

955 WHITE THORN LODGE
RD #1, Box 242 (412)846-5984
☐ Darlington, PA 96115 PR+MH+CRV

A 106-acre, member-owned nudist park located in western Pennsylvania near the Ohio state line, 50 miles from downtown Pittsburg. Elevation 1,000 ft. Open for visitors May through September.

The outdoor hot tub using electrically-heated well water treated with bromine is maintained at 105º. The swimming pool, using sun-heated well water treated with bromine, varies in temperature. Nudity is expected, weather permitting, everywhere on the grounds.

Facilities include hiking trails, rooms, RV hook-ups, camping spaces, clubhouse, sauna, weekend snackbar, tennis and volleyball courts, horseshoe pits, junior clubhouse and play area. No credit cards are accepted.

Note: This is a membership organization not open to the public for drop-in visits, but interested visitors may be issued a guest pass by prior arrangement. Telephone or write for information and directions.

957   THE GREENBRIER   (800) 624-6070
(304) 536-1110
White Sulphur Springs, WV 24986   MH

A large, historic, health-oriented mineral spring resort occupying 6,500 acres in an upland valley of the Allegheny Mountains, near the Virginia border. Elevation 2,900 ft. Open all year.

Natural mineral water flows out of a sulphur spring at 58º and is piped to individual soaking tubs in separate men's and women's sections of the mineral-bath wing, where it is heated by electricity to the desired temperature. Tubs are drained and filled after each use so that no chemical treatment is needed. Water from a fresh-water spring is piped to an outdoor pool and to the *Grand Indoor Pool*, where it is treated with chlorine and heated by steam to a temperature of 75º. Bathing suits are required.

Facilities include rooms and luxury suites, dining rooms and restaurants, a complete convention center, shops, service station, tennis courts, three golf courses, aerobics studio, exercise equipment, beauty salon and a complete diagnostic clinic. Services include fitness evaluations, massage, herbal wrap, facials, manicures and pedicures. The diagnostic clinic and shops are available to the public. All other facilities are for the use of registered guests only. Visa, MasterCard, American Express and Diners Club are accepted. Phone or write for rates, reservations and directions.

The Greenbrier offers medical diagnostic services plus recreational opportunities such as this elegant indoor pool.

958   THE HOMESTEAD

Hot Springs, VA 24445

(703) 839-5500

MH

A very large, very historic, luxurious resort on the west slope of the Alleghany Mountains near the West Virginia Border. Elevation 2,500 ft. Open all year.

The odorless mineral water used at the Homestead Spa flows from several springs at temperatures ranging from 102º to 106º. It is piped to individual, one-person bathtubs in separate men's and women's bathhouses, where it is mixed to provide an ideal temperature of 104º. Tubs are drained and refilled after each use so that no chemical treatment of the water is necessary. Mineral water from the same springs is used in an indoor swimming pool maintained at 84º and an outdoor swimmming pool maintained at 72º. Both pools receive a minimum of chlorine treatment. Use of the spa and all pools is restricted to registered guests only. Bathing suits are required except as indicated in the bathhouses.

Five miles away but still within the 15,000-acre Homestead property are the Warm Springs, which flow at 96º. The rate of discharge is so great that the two large Warms Springs pools, in separate men's and women's buildings, maintain a temperature of 96º on a flow-through basis requiring no chemical treatment of the water. These Warm Springs' pools are open only during the warm months and are open to the public. Bathing suits are optional.

The facilites include 600 bedrooms and parlors, restaurants, shops, conference center, bowling alley, movie theatre and tennis courts. Recreational activities available on the premises include golf, archery, fishing, hiking, riding, skeet and trap shooting and tennis, plus skiing and ice skating in the winter. There are many resort services available, some of which are included in the basic room rate. Phone or write for complete information. Visa, MasterCard and American Express are accepted.

The Homestead: An abundance of hot mineral water enables this famous resort to offer several indoor and outdoor swimming pools in addition to traditional tubs in men's and women's bathhouses.

959　WHITE TAIL PARK

☐

P.O. Box 160　　　　　(804) 859-6123
Zuni, VA 23898　　　　PR+MH+CRV

Large (47-acre), well-equipped family nudist park located in southeastern Virginia, 35 miles from I-95 and 45 miles from Norfolk. Elevation 39 ft. Open all year.

A large, indoor spa/hot tub filled with gas-heated well water, treated with bromine, and is maintained at 104º. The outdoor swimming pool is filled with solar-heated well water, treated with Baquacil, and maintained in the low 80's from April to November. This is a nudist resort, so everyone is expected to be nude, weather and health permitting.

Facilities include 17 mobile home living sites, nature trail, recreation hall, children's rec center, game courts, rooms, tenting spaces, RV hookups and seasonal snack bar. Visa and MasterCard are accepted. It is four miles to all other services.

Note: This is a membership organization, but the park will accept drop-in visitors anytime. Telephone or write for information and directions.

960　HOT SPRINGS SPA

■

P.O. Box 428　　　　　(704) 622-7676
Hot Springs, NC 28743　　PR+CRV

Picturesque rustic spa and campground on the banks of the French Broad River, in the mountains near the Tennessee border. Elevation 2,000 feet. Open all year.

Natural mineral water flows out of a spring at 100º and is piped to six outdoor soaking pools scattered through a wooded area along the river. Pools are drained and refilled after each use so that no chemical treatment of the water is required. One of the pools is equipped with a plastic bubble for winter use. Bathing suits are officially required, but some of the pools are very secluded.

Facilities include RV hookups and a service station. Massage is available on the premises. All other services are available 1/4 mile away in the town. Visa and MasterCard are accepted.

Phone for rates, reservations and directions.

961　ROCK HAVEN LODGE

☐

P.O. Box 1291　　　　　(615) 896-3553
Murfreesboro, TN 37133　　PR+MH+CRV

A traditional, family nudist park with a country atmosphere, located on 25 wooded acres, 40 miles from Nashville. Elevation 650 ft. Open for visitors April 1 to October 31.

One large, outdoor whirlpool spa using chlorine-treated well water is maintained at 103º, and one outdoor unheated swimming pool using similar water averages over 70º in the summer. Clothing is prohibited in pools. This is a nudist park, not a clothing-optional resort, so members and guests are expected to be nude, weather permitting.

Facilities include rental cabins, RV hookups, camping area, clubhouse, volleyball, tennis and other sports courts. No credit cards are accepted. It is six miles to stores, restaurants and motels.

Note: This is a membership organization, but the park will accept drop-in first-time visitors anytime. Telephone or write for information and directions.

962　HIDDEN VALLEY

☐

Rt. 3, Box 3452　　　　(404) 476-8955
Dawsonville, GA 30534　　PR+MH+CRV

A secluded, heavily wooded nudist resort nestled in the scenic foothills of the North Georgia Mountains. Elevation 1,500 ft. Open mid-March through early December.

Gas-heated well water, treated with bromine and chlorine, is used in an enclosed outdoor hydropool which comfortably holds 12 and is maintained at 104º. A spacious cement-and-rock-lined pond, fed by a running mountain stream, maintains a temperature of 65º. Clothing is prohibited in both pools. This is a nudist club, not a clothing-optional resort, so nudity is generally expected everywhere, weather permitting.

Facilities include rental rooms and housekeeping units, RV spaces, camping area, seasonal snack bar, volleyball, tennis and shuffleboard courts. Visa and MasterCard are accepted. It is five miles to a store and restaurant.

This is a family-oriented club which accepts singles on a reservation basis only. Membership is not required to visit, and couples and families may visit without making reservations. Phone or write for further information and directions.

971 SUNNY SANDS RESORT

502 Central Blvd.　　　　(904) 749-2233
Pierson, FL 32080　　　　PR+MH+CRV

Fifty acres of rustic woods surrounding a private lake, located 20 miles north of Deland in northeastern Florida. Elevation 20 ft. Open all year.

The outdoor hydrojet spa is filled with gas-heated well water, treated with bromine, and maintained at 103º. The swimming pool is filled with heated well water, treated with chlorine, and varies in temperature with the seasons. Clothing is prohibited in the pools, and nudity is expected elsewhere, weather and health permitting.

Facilities include mobile-home rentals, RV hook-ups, tenting spaces, recreation hall, fishing, volleyball and shuffleboard courts, horseshoe pit and playground. Visa and MasterCard are accepted. It is 20 miles to Deland and all other services.

Note: This is a membership organization open for drop-in visits by couples or families. Telephone or write for more information and directions.

972 CYPRESS COVE NUDIST RESORT

4425 Pleasant Hill Rd　　　(407) 933-5870
Kissimmee, FL 34746　　　PR+MH+CRV

Beautiful large modern clothing-free destination resort surrounding a private 50 acre lake, in central Florida, within 30 minutes of Disney World, Cypress Gardens and Sea World. As this is a family resort, most visitors are married couples, many with children. Singles are also welcomed when accompanied by a member of the opposite sex. Elevation 77 feet. Open all year.

Well water, heated by gas, is piped to two outdoor pools. The whirlpool spa is heated to 103º and treated with bromine. The swimming pool is heated to 80º and treated with chlorine. Nudity is expected in the pool areas, everyone dresses for the Saturday night dances, and clothing is optional at other times and places, according to comfort and to suit the occasion.

Motel rooms, apartments, RV spaces, restaurant, poolside bar, and paddleboats for the lake are available on the premises. Activities such as exercise and yoga classes, tennis clinics, craft classes and Coffee Klatch Hours are also available. It is eight miles to a service station and market. Visa and MasterCard are accepted.

Directions: South of Orlando, follow US 17-92 three miles south of Kissimmee to FL 531 (Pleasant Hill Road). Turn left eight miles to Cypress Cove.

973 RESORT AND SPA AT WARM MINERAL SPRINGS

San Servando Ave.　　　(813) 426-9581
Warm Mineral Springs, FL 34287 PR+MH

Modern spa, health studio and nearby apartment complex, with a nine-million-gallons-per-day mineral spring, located halfway between Ft. Meyers and Sarasota. Elevation 10 ft. Open all year.

Mineral water flows out of the ground at 87º into a two-acre private lake and is also piped to a health studio. The lake, which is used for swimming, does not need chlorination because of the volume of flow-through mineral water. The indoor soaking tubs and whirlpool baths are filled with 87º water. The tubs are drained and refilled after each use so that no chemical treatment is needed. Bathing suits are required except in private rooms.

Facilities include sauna, gift shop, post office, bakery and snack bar. Massage, hot pack, medical examinations and rental of nearby apartments are available on the premises. No credit cards are accepted. Phone for rates, reservations and directions.

SAVE WATER

BATHe WITH A FRIEND

974   CITY RETREAT NUDIST PARK

13220 Houston Ave.   (813) 868-1061
☐   Hudson, FL 34667   PR+MH+CRV

Forty acres of tree-shaded nudist tranquility in a grassy-sandy country setting, 45 miles north of Tampa. Elevation 30 ft. Open all year.

The outdoor hydrospa is filled with gas-heated well water treated with chlorine, and maintained at 101-103º. The outdoor pool is filled with heated well water maintained at 82º and treated with chlorine. Clothing is prohibited in the pool and spa area. This is a nudist club, not a clothing-optional resort. Clothing is not allowed in the pool area. Everyone dresses according to the weather.

Facilities include a club house, motel rooms, campers, mobile homes, tenting spaces, RV hook-ups, snack bar, tennis court, and shuffleboard courts. Visa and MasterCard are accepted. It is five miles to a shopping center.

Note: We are family oriented; however anyone with a sincere interest in nudism is welcome. Phone for information, rates and directions.

▲ *City Retreat Nudist Park:* Traditional nudist parks do have clothing rules; it is prohibited in the pools and pool area.

975   SAFETY HARBOR SPA AND FITNESS CENTER

105 N. Bayshore Dr.   1-800-237-0155
■   Safety Harbor, FL 34695   PR+MH

An upscale historic spa, recently refurbished, specializing in fitness and beauty programs, located at the west end of Tampa Bay. Elevation 10ft. Open all year.

Natural mineral water flows from four springs at approximately 55º and is piped to several pools and to separate men's and women's bathhouses. Gas is used to heat the water as needed. The six individual soaking tubs in the men's and ladies bathhouses are drained and filled after each use so no chemical treatment of the water is necessary. All other pools are treated with chlorine. The courtyard swimming pool, the lap pool, the indoor exercise pool and the ladies' pool are maintained at 85º. Two coed hydrojet pools are maintained at 99º and 101º. Bathing suits are not required in bathhouses.

Facilities include fitness center, tennis courts, golf driving range, guest rooms, dining room and conference center. Tennis and golf lessons, excercise classes, medical and nutritional consultation, massage, herbal wraps, skin care treatment and complete beauty salon services are available on the premises. All facilities and services are reserved for the use of registered guests only. Visa, MasterCard, American Express, and Diner Club are accepted.

Phone for rates, reservations and directions.

976   ETHOS TRACE, INC.

5000 Guernsey Rd.   (904) 994-9160
☐   Pace, FL 32571   PR+ CRV

A sixteen acre tree-shaded family-oriented nudist park, located near Pensacola and I-10 in the Florida panhandle. Elevation 120 feet. Open all year.

The outdoor hydrojet spa and swimming pool are filled with gas-heated city water treated with chlorine. The spa is maintained at 102º and the swimming pool at 78º, with a plastic dome available for wintertime comfort. This is a nudist park, so members and visitors are expected to be nude, weather permitting.

Facilities include RV hook-ups, camping spaces, lighted volleyball courts, horseshoe pits and sunning lawns. No credit cards are accepted. All other services are available within five miles.

Interested visitors are welcome. A daily "ground fee" entitles each visitor to use the pools and all other recreational facilities. Phone for rates, reservations and directions.

▲
▶
▼ *Safety Harbor Spa and Fitness Center:*
These deluxe pools and accomodations,
plus beauty and fitness services, are
about as different as you can get from a
primitive wilderness hot spring.

The opportunity to "soak in peace" has drawn humankind to this Hot Spring Mountain for thousands of years. Hernando De Soto may or may not have been the first European on the scene, but today's Hot Springs National Park, and the surrounding community, have their roots in the 1803 Louisiana Purchase. In 1832 Congress took the unprecedented step of establishing public ownership by setting aside four sections of land as a reservation. Unfortunately, no one adequately identified the exact boundaries of this reservation, so the mid-19th century was filled with conflicting claims and counterclaims to the springs and surrounding land.

By 1870 a system evolved that reserved the springs for the Federal Government and sold the developed land to the persons who had settled it. At the same time the government agreed to collect the $143°$ geothermal spring water into a central distribution system which carried it to private property establishments where baths were offered to the public. By 1877 all primitive soaking "pits" along Hot Springs Creek were eliminated when the creek was confined to a concrete channel, roofed over, and then paved to create what is now Central Avenue.

In 1921 the Federal Reservation became Hot Springs National Park, custodian of all the springs, and the exclusive contractual supplier of hot mineral water to those elaborate establishments which had become the famous Bathhouse Row. It is also the authority which aproves every establishment's rates, equipment, personnel and services related to that water.

Until 1949 each bathhouse needed to have its own evaporation tower in order to cool the incoming hot mineral water to a tolerable temperature for human skin. In that year the Park Service installed air-cooled radiators and tap-water cooled heat exchangers to supply a new central "cool" mineral water reservoir. Now all thermal water customers receive their suppy through two pipes, "hot" at $143°$ and "cool" at $90°$.

During the last four decades declining patronage has forced the closure of most of those historic temples for "taking the waters." However, resort hotels, motels and therapy centers in downtown Hot Springs have responded to increasing demands for thermal soaking, and some of the historic Bathhouse Row locations are being refurbished and reopened. For additional information, write to the Hot Springs Chamber of Commerce, P.O. Box 1500, Hot Springs, AR 71902.

Two of the hot springs in the park have been left uncovered, for visitor observation only. There is a campground for tents and trailers but it does not have electrical or water connections.

The BUCKSTAFF BATHHOUSE and the LIBBEY MEMORIAL PHYSICAL MEDICINE CENTER AND HOT SPRINGS HEALTH SPA are concessioners located in Hot Springs National Park. All of the other locations described below operate in the adjacent city, under National Park regulations as a condition for receiving geothermal water through the Park's distribution system. Each establishment has its own pohone number for information, rates and reservations.

991A   BUCKSTAFF BATHS

■   (501) 623-2308

One of the historic Bathhouse Row establishments in continuous operation since 1912, located at the south end of the Row near the Visitor Center.

Separate men's and women's sections offer one-person soaking tubs which are individually temperature-controlled. They are drained and refilled after each use so no chemical treatment of the water is needed. Whirlpool baths and massage are available.

Facilities include a third-floor coed lounge with separate men's and women's sun decks at each end. No credit cards are accepted.

991B LIBBEY MEMORIAL PHYSICAL MEDICINE CENTER AND HOT SPRINGS HEALTH SPA

■ (501) 321-1997

Downstairs, a modern, "Medicare-Approved, Federally Regulated" therapy facility and, upstairs, a modern spa with coed soaking tubs, located on Reserve Avenue, three blocks east of Central Avenue.

The Libbey Memorial coed thermal whirlpool (105º) and coed exercise pool (98º) are drained and refilled each day, so no chemical treatment of the water is necessary. Facilities include steam and vapor cabinets and electric hoists at therapy pools. Hot packs, massage and prescribed treatments such as Paraffin Immersion, Ultra Sound Therapy, and Electric Stimulation are also available. No credit cards are accepted.

The Health Spa's eight large coed soaking tubs are individually temperature-controlled as desired between 102º and 108º. All of them are drained and filled each day so that no chemical treatment of the water is necessary. Children are welcome. Massage, steam and vapor cabinets, sunbeds and exercise equipment are available. No credit cards are accepted.

Libbey Hot Springs Health Spa: These large coed pools available on the second floor are highly popular with families.

991C ARLINGTON RESORT HOTEL & SPA

1 (800) 643-1502
Arkansas (501) 623-7771

A magnificent, luxurious resort in a dominant location overlooking Central Avenue and Bathhouse Row.

The in-hotel bathhouse with separate men's and women's sections is open to the public. Private soaking tubs are individually temperature-controlled and drained after each use so that no chemical treatment of the water is necessary. Massage, hot packs, saunas, sitz-baths and needle showers are available.

A mineral-water redwood hot tub, two tap water swimming pools treated with chlorine, and a multi-level sundeck are reserved for registered guests. The hot tub is maintained at 104º, and the twin pools are maintained at 86º year round.

Facilities include three restaurants and two lounges, beauty salon, exercise room, ballroom, conference and exhibit centers, VIP Club and shopping mall. Visa, MasterCard, American Express, and Discover are accepted.

Arlington Resort Hotel and Spa: Deluxe amenities, including poolside service , are part of the tradition established by this famous destination resort and spa.

991D DOWNTOWNER HOTEL & SPA

(501) 624-5521

A modern motor lodge with a large second-floor bathhouse, located on Central Avenue one block north of Bathhouse Row.

A bathhouse with separate men's and women's sections is open to the public. One-person soaking tubs are individually temperature-controlled and drained after each use so that no chemical treatment of the water is necessary. Whirlpool baths, vapor treatments, hot packs, sitz baths and massage are available.

An outdoor swimming pool and a hot tub are filled with chlorine-treated tap water, and are reserved for the use of registered guests.

Facilities include a beauty salon, sun decks and two restaurants. Visa, MasterCard, American Express and Discover are accepted.

991E HOT SPRINGS HILTON

1 (800) HILTONS
Arkansas (501) 623-6600

Large, modern, resort hotel located next to the Hot Springs Convention Center, two blocks south of Bathhouse Row.

A bathhouse with separate men's and women's sections is open to the public. One-person soaking tubs are individually temperature-controlled and drained after each use so that no chemical treatment of the water is necessary. Massage is available.

An indoor whirlpool (108º) and an indoor-outdoor swimming pool filled with chlorine-treated tap water are reserved for the use of registered guests.

Facilities include restaurants, lounge, meeting rooms and banquet facilities. Visa, MasterCard, American Express, Diners Club and Discover are accepted.

Hot Springs Hilton: Spotless tile and chrome decorate the bathhouse tubs and the indoor access pool for swimmers.

991F MAJESTIC RESORT/SPA

1 (800) 643-1504
Arkansas (501) 623-5511

A unique combination of hotel, motel and health spa facilities located at the north end of Central Avenue.

A bathhouse with separate men's and women's sections is open to the public. Individual soaking tubs are temperature-controlled and drained after each use so that no chemical treatment of the water is necessary. Massage is available.

An outdoor swimming pool filled with chlorine-treated tap water and heated in the winter is reserved for the use of registered guests.

Facilities include deluxe rooms and suites, beauty salon, two restaurants and a lounge, ole' fashioned soda fountain, gift and clothing shops, conference and banquet rooms. Visa, MasterCard, American Express and Discover are accepted.

992A EXCELSIOR SPRINGS MINERAL WATER SPA

Hall Of Waters   **(816) 637-0753**
Excelsior Springs, MO 64024   **PR**

A large, historic building originally constructed for health-oriented activities is now owned and operated on a limited scale by the city. Elevation 900 ft. Open weekdays only.

Cold (54º) natural mineral water is pumped from wells (which used to be flowing springs) and piped to a bathhouse where it is gas-heated and used in four individual, private-space tubs. After each use they are drained and refilled so that no chemical treatment of the water is necessary. The bathhouse is for men only in the morning and women only in the afternoon. Steambaths and massage are available on the premises. The indoor swimming pool, using gas-heated, chlorine-treated tap water is maintained at approximately 75º and open only in the summer. Bathing suits are required in this coed pool.

Facilities include dressing rooms and a water bar, where mineral water is sold by the gallon. Visa and MasterCard are accepted. Phone for rates, reservations and directions.

Elms Resort Hotel: Although mineral water is used only in the New Leaf Spa small tubs, this location has many other hot water pools; one even has a waterfall.

992B THE ELMS RESORT HOTEL

Regent and Elms Blvd.   **(816) 637-2141**
Excelsior Springs, MO 64024   **PR+MH**

An historic luxury resort on 23 wooded acres, a half-hour northeast of Kansas City. Elevation 900 ft. Open all year.

Cold (54º) natural mineral water is pumped from wells on the property and piped to single soaking tubs in separate men's and women's section of the elaborate New Leaf Spa. Customers control tub water temperature by adding hot tap water to the cold mineral water as desired. The tubs are drained and filled after each use so no chemical treatment of the water is necessary.

Chlorine-treated tap water, is used in all other pools. There are two theme rooms, each containing environmental effects and a two-person soaking tub in which water temperature is controllable. The indoor European swimming track is maintained at 75º, the three large, outdoor hot tub pools are maintained at 100º, and the outdoor swimming pool is solar heated. Bathing suits are required in these public-area coed pools. The New Leaf Spa is open to the public as well as to registered guests.

New Leaf Spa services include steambaths, jogging track, saunas, beauty shop, exercise room, herbal wrap and massage. Other facilities include rooms, suites, condos, restaurant, and various sports courts. Visa, MasterCard, American Express and Diners Club are accepted. Phone for rates, reservations and directions.

993 THE ORIGINAL MINERAL SPRINGS HOTEL AND BATH HOUSE
(618) 243-5458

■ **Okawville, IL 62271**

An authentic turn-of-the-century mineral spring resort hotel, located in a small town on I-64, 40 miles east of St. Louis. Elevation 600 ft. Open all year.

Natural mineral water flows out of a spring at approximately 50º and is piped to separate men's and women's bathhouses where it is gas-heated as needed in one-person soaking tubs. Tubs are drained and filled after each use so no chemical treatment of the water is necessary. The indoor/outdoor swimming pool uses gas-heated tap water treated with chlorine, and is maintained at 85º. Bathing suits are not required in bathhouses. Day use customers are welcome.

Facilities include guest rooms and a restaurant. Massage is available on the premises. Visa, MasterCard, Discover and American Express are accepted. It is less than four blocks to a service station, store and other services.

Phone for rates, reservations and directions.

994 FRENCH LICK SPRINGS RESORT
(812) 936-9300

■ **French Lick, IN 47432**   **PR+MH**

The "Largest Most Complete Resort in the Midwest," located on 2600 wooded acres in southwest Indiana, two hours from Indianapolis. Elevation 600 ft. Open all year.

Natural mineral water flows from a spring at 50º and is piped to separate men's and women's bathhouses where it is heated by gas-generated steam, as needed, into one-person soaking tubs. Tubs are drained and filled after each use so no chemical treatment of the water is necessary. All other pools use steam-heated tap water treated with chlorine. The outdoor and indoor whirlpools are maintained at 104º, the dome pool ranges from 72º in the summer to 82º in the winter, and the Olympic swimming pool, for summer use only, is not heated. Bathing suits are required except in bathhouses.

Facilities include two 18-hole golf courses, indoor and outdoor tennis courts, equestrian stables and riding trails, guest rooms, nine restaurants and lounges, bowling alleys, conference center, exercise facility and beauty salon. Massage, body treatments, saunas, steambaths, reflexology, salt rubs, facials and manicures are available on the premises. Visa, MasterCard and American Express are accepted. It is three blocks to a service station, store and other services.

Phone for rates, reservations and directions.

995 WHISPERING OAKS
5864 Baldwin   (313) 628-2676
☐   Oxford, MI 48371   PR+CRV

A traditional nudist resort on 52 acres of beautiful rolling woodland with a private lake, 35 miles north of Detroit. Elevation 1,200 ft. Open from April to October.

The outdoor whirlpool spa is filled with propane-heated well water, treated with chlorine, and maintained at 105º. The outdoor diving pool is filled with propane-heated well water, treated with chlorine, and maintained at 80º. This is a nudist facility, so everyone is expected to be nude weather and health permitting.

Facilities include sauna, clubhouse, RV hook-ups, tenting spaces, and volleyball, tennis and shuffleboard courts. Visa and MasterCard are accepted. It is five miles to a service station, cafe and motel.

Note: This is a membership organization not open to the public for drop-in visits, but prospective members may be issued a guest pass by prior arrangement. Telephone or write for information and directions.

Welcome to our OOL — Notice there is no P in it — Please keep it that way

996 CLEARWATER HOT TUBS

1201 Butterfield Rd.　　(708) 852-7676
Downers Grove, IL 60515　　　　PR

A user-friendly, rent-a-tub facility located in a suburban town 25 miles west of Chicago.

Private space redwood hot tubs using gas-heated tap water are treated with bromine. Four of the the twelve units are VIP suites with TV and oversized tubs, suitable for large groups. Eleven have a sauna, and a sensory deprivation flotation tank is available in the twelfth. Pool temperatures are maintained at approximately 100º in the summer and 104º in the winter. Clothing is optional in the private spaces and required elsewhere.

Massage is available by appointment. Visa, MasterCard, American Express, and Discover Card are accepted. Phone for rates, reservations and directions.

Clearwater Hot Tubs: Modern rent-a-tub establishments have responded to customer's demands by providing pools large enough to accomodate a whole family or recreational group.

EVANS PLUNGE
(not shown on any key map)
1145 North River　　(605) 745-5165
Hot Springs, SD 57747　　　　PR

The world's largest natural warm water indoor swimming pool and water park, located at the north edge of the town of Hot Springs, in southwestern South Dakota. Elevation 3,800 feet. Open all year.

5,000 gallons per minute of 87º water rises out of the pebble bottom of the Plunge, providing a complete change of water 16 times daily, so only a minimum of chlorine is necessary. Waterslides, traveling rings, fun tubes, and kiddie pools are available at the Plunge. Two hydrojet spas (100º - 104º), sauna, steam room, and fitness equipment are located in the Health Club. No credit cards are accepted.

A gift shop is available on the premises. All other services are available within 1/2 mile.

The **American Sunbathing Association** is a 50-year old national nudist organization which is the U.S. representative in the International Naturist Federation. The A.S.A. annualy publishes a Nudist Park Guide, containing complete information about nudism and all of the local parks and clubs. The A.S.A. also publishes informational pamphlets which are free for the asking. Send your inquiry to:

American Sunbathing Association
1703 North Main St. Kissimmee, FL 32743

The **Naturist Society**, which started as a free beach movement, has expanded its goals to include legalization of nude swimming and sunbathing on designated public land, including parks and forests as well as beaches. It offers individual membership and publishes a quarterly journal about clothing optional opportunities. If you would like to know more, address your inquiry to:

The Naturist Society
P.O. Box 132, Oshkosh, WI 54902

Alphabetical Master Index

This index is designed to help you locate a listing when you start with the location name. The description of the location will be found on the page number given for that name.

Within the index the abbreviations listed below are used to identify the specific state or geographical area of the location. The number shown after each state listed below is the page number where the KEY MAP of that state will be found.

AB=Alberta, Canada / 31
AK=Alaska / 22
BC=British Columbia, Canada / 30
ES=Eastern States / 174
ID=Idaho / 86
MT=Montana / 150
OR=Oregon / 64
WA=Washington / 52
WY=Wyoming / 160

NUBP=Not Usable By the Public

MIETTE HOT SPRINGS   AB 36
MILE 16 HOT SPRING *see*
  SUGAH HOT SPRING   ID 144
MIRACLE HOT SPRINGS   ID 121
MOLLY'S HOT SPRING   ID 143
MOLLY'S TUBS   ID 142
MOON DIPPER HOT SPRINGS   ID 139
MOUNT LAYTON HOT SPRINGS RESORT   BC 35
MURPHY'S HOT SPRINGS   ID 123

NAKUSP HOT SPRINGS   BC 45
NAT-SOO-PAH HOT SPRINGS   ID 119
NEINMEYER HOT SPRINGS   ID 131
NOTARAS LODGE   WA 54

OLYMPIC HOT SPRINGS   WA 61
ONSEN HOT TUB RENTALS   OR 76
OPEN AIR HOT TUBBING   OR 85
ORIGINAL MINERAL SPRINGS   ES 189
OWEN CABIN HOT SPRINGS   ID 96

PINE BURL HOT SPRINGS   ID 139
PINE FLATS HOT SPRING   ID 136
PISTOL CREEK HOT SPRINGS   ID 96
PLAZA HOTEL AND APARTMENTS   WY 163
PREIS HOT SPRING   ID 109

QUINN'S PARADISE RESORT   MT 158

RADIUM HOT SPRINGS   BC 41
RED RIVER HOT SPRINGS   ID 87
RESORT AND SPA AT WARM
  MINERAL SPRINGS   ES 181
RIGGINS HOT SPRINGS   ID 149
RIVERDALE RESORT   ID 116
RIVERSIDE INN   ID 115
ROCK HAVEN LODGE   ES 180
ROCKY CANYON HOT SPRING   ID 138
ROOSEVELT BATH HOUSE   ES 176
RUSSIAN JOHN HOT SPRING   ID 106

SACAJAWEA HOT SPRINGS   ID 132
SAFETY HARBOR SPA   ES 182
SALMON HOT SPRING   ID 97
SAND SPRINGS POOL   ES 175
SARATOGA INN   WY 164
SAWTOOTH LODGE   ID 132
SCENIC HOT SPRINGS   WA 54
SHARKEY HOT SPRING   ID 98
SHEEP CREEK BRIDGE HOT SPRINGS   ID 131
SHOSHONE GEYSER BAISIN   WY 172
SHOWER BATH HOT SPRINGS   ID 96
SILVER CREEK PLUNGE   ID 140
SKILLERN HOT SPRINGS   ID 109
SKOOKUMCHUCK HOT SPRINGS   BC 48
SLATE CREEK HOT SPRING   ID 102
SLEEPING CHILD HOT SPRINGS   MT 156
SLIGAR'S THOUSAND SPRINGS RESORT   ID 122
SLOQUET CREEK HOT SPRINGS   BC 49

SMITH CABIN HOT SPRINGS   ID 131
SNIVELY HOT SPRINGS   OR 66
SOLAIR RECREATION LEAGUE   ES 176
SOL DUC HOT SPRINGS   WA 62
SPA OF AMHERST   ES 175
SPA MOTEL   MT 153
SPRINGFIELD SPAS   OR 76
ST. MARTINS ON THE WIND   WA 56
STANLEY HOT SPRING   ID 88
STAR PLUNGE   WY 163
STATE BATH HOUSE   WY 162
SUGAH HOT SPRING   ID 144
SULLIVAN HOT SPRINGS   omitted by
  owner's request
SUMMER LAKE HOT SPRINGS   OR 69
SUNBEAM HOT SPRINGS   ID 103
SUNFLOWER FLATS HOT SPRINGS   ID 94
SUNNY CHINOOKS FAMILY NUDIST
  RECREATIONAL PARK   AB 37
SUNNY SANDS RESORT   ES 181
SYMES HOTEL AND MEDICINAL SPRINGS   MT 159

TAKHINI HOT SPRINGS   AK 32
TENAKEE HOT SPRINGS   AK 28
TERWILIGER HOT SPRINGS   OR 75
TOLOVANA HOT SPRINGS   AK 25
TOWN TUBS AND MASSAGE   WA 58
TRAIL CREEK HOT SPRING *see*
  BREIT HOT SPRING   ID 138
TUBS BELLEVUE   WA 59
TUBS SEATTLE   WA 60
TWIN SPRINGS RESORT   ID (NUBP)

UMPQUA WARM SPRING   OR 70
UPPER HOT SPRINGS   AB 39

VULCAN HOT SPRINGS   ID 144

WALL CREEK WARM SPRING *see*
  MEDITATION POOL   OR 74
WARFIELD HOT SPRING   ID 105
WARM SPRINGS RESORT   ID 125
WASHAKIE HOT SPRINGS   WY (NUBP)
WATERHOLE LODGE   ID 147
WEIR CREEK HOT SPRINGS   ID 88
WELLSPRING   WA 56
WEST PASS HOT SPRING   ID 101
WHISPERING OAKS   ES 189
WHITE ARROW HOT SPRINGS   ID (NUBP)
WHITE LICKS HOT SPRINGS   ID 146
WHITEHORSE RANCH HOT SPRING   OR 67
WHITE SULPHER HOT SPRINGS   AK 29
WHITE TAIL PARK   ES 180
WHITE THORN LODGE   ES 177
WHITEY COX HOT SPRINGS   ID 95
WILLOW CREEK HOT SPRINGS   ID 111
WORSWICK HOT SPRINGS   ID 108

ZIM'S HOT SPRINGS   ID 148

BOOK MAIL ORDER

Name

Street

City   State   Zip

Each book: $14.95 + $2.00 shipping = $16.95

	Order Quan.	Amount
Hot Springs and Hot Pools of the Northwest	$16.95	
Hot Springs and Hot Pools of the Southwest	$16.95	
Day Trips in Nature: CALIFORNIA	$16.95	
		TOTAL

Make check to: AQUA THERMAL ACCESS
Mail to: 55 Azalea Lane, Santa Cruz, CA 95060

BOOK MAIL ORDER

Name

Street

City   State   Zip

Each book: $14.95 + $2.00 shipping = $16.95

	Order Quan.	Amount
Hot Springs and Hot Pools of the Northwest	$16.95	
Hot Springs and Hot Pools of the Southwest	$16.95	
Day Trips in Nature: CALIFORNIA	$16.95	
		TOTAL

Make check to: AQUA THERMAL ACCESS
Mail to: 55 Azalea Lane, Santa Cruz, CA 95060

Form 1

Name

Street

City _____ State _____ Zip

	Order Quan.	Amount
Each book: $14.95 + $2.00 shipping = $16.95		
Hot Springs and Hot Pools of the Northwest — $16.95		
Hot Springs and Hot Pools of the Southwest — $16.95		
Day Trips in Nature: CALIFORNIA — $16.95		
		TOTAL

BOOK MAIL ORDER   Make check to: AQUA THERMAL ACCESS   Mail to: 55 Azalea Lane, Santa Cruz, CA 95060

Form 2

Name

Street

City _____ State _____ Zip

	Order Quan.	Amount
Each book: $14.95 + $2.00 shipping = $16.95		
Hot Springs and Hot Pools of the Northwest — $16.95		
Hot Springs and Hot Pools of the Southwest — $16.95		
Day Trips in Nature: CALIFORNIA — $16.95		
		TOTAL

BOOK MAIL ORDER   Make check to: AQUA THERMAL ACCESS   Mail to: 55 Azalea Lane, Santa Cruz, CA 95060